WHAT DOES IT MEAN WHEN YOU DREAM ABOUT . . .

mirrors? • flying? • .pain? • the ocean? • fruit? • pregnancy?
the number seven? • the number twelve? • birds? • the moon?
a hotel? • diamonds? • the color orange? • sex? • angels? • fire? • light?

Now You Can Find Out . . .

with this simple, practical guide including dream symbols from the common to the unusual—and helpful tips for remembering, understanding, and benefiting from your dreams!

THE DREAM DICTIONARY
1,000 Dream Symbols From A to Z

★ THE ★
DREAM
DICTIONARY
1,000
DREAM SYMBOLS FROM
A ★ TO ★ Z

JO ● JEAN ● BOUSHAHLA ● AND
VIRGINIA ● REIDEL–GEUBTNER

B

BERKLEY BOOKS, NEW YORK

This Berkley book contains the complete text
of the original hardcover edition.

THE DREAM DICTIONARY

A Berkley Book / published by arrangement with
Pilgrim Press / The United Church Board for Homeland Ministries

PRINTING HISTORY
Pilgrim Press edition published 1983
Berkley trade paperback edition / February 1992

ISBN: 0-425-13190-4

A BERKLEY BOOK® TM 757,375
Berkley Books are published by The Berkley Publishing Group,
200 Madison Avenue, New York, New York 10016.
The name "BERKLEY" and the "B" logo
are trademarks belonging to Berkley Publishing Corporation.

PRINTED IN THE UNITED STATES OF AMERICA

10 9 8 7 6 5 4 3

*To Bob, Lynn, Carol, Lori, and Bettye Dale
who have and always will share my dreams.*
—J.B.

To Michael, Gabrielle, and Justin.
—V.G.

Contents

Acknowledgments

This book presents a collection of symbols started over a decade ago, as the outcome of a dream study group. Other members came and went but, dedicated and enthusiastic, we two authors remained. Two years ago, we decided to put the fruit of our research into book form. For their encouragement at the outset, we want to express our thanks to Dr. Herbert Bruce Puryear and the late Hugh Lynn Cayce. To Dr. Mark Thurston, our deepest gratitude for answering questions and helping us with ideas on how to make the book more complete, as well as allowing us to quote from his *How to Interpret Your Dreams.*

To our families, who listened as we read sections to them and responded to our requests by suggesting fresh ways to improve and clarify our writing, we are extremely thankful.

Our thanks to Lorie Skalland whose mathematical expertise was a positive influence on the Numbers chapter.

And finally to Robert Iles who did some editing for us, our appreciation for his time, consideration, and, most of all, his objectivity.

Jo Jean Boushahla
Virginia Reidel-Geubtner

February 1983

Introduction:
Dreams, Visions,
and Symbols

Quietly and wordlessly, proof of the ancient Chinese saying that "one picture is worth a thousand words" has existed for eons in the symbols used in religious cultures around the world. We presently experiment with drugs, alcohol, and biofeedback when exploring the inner world of the human body. Because dreams are commonplace, many people belittle their importance in comparison to other, more unusual and expensive methods of consciousness expansion. If we are wise, we will appreciate the experience that is given freely each night. In our personal, inner search, working with dreams is not just a starting point but a main vehicle for self discovery. Dreams help us to understand where we are and become who we are.

Dreams and visions are considered interchangeable in this book because each comes from the same source (see Spiritual Centers chart). True, a vision is a waking experience, but some dreams are also of a visionary nature. The symbols and feeling-tones of both indicate that they come from a high level of consciousness, and they are treated accordingly throughout the book. They are the activity of the real self, transforming outer activities into an inner experience conveying a message; transformation takes place from the instinctive animal level to the higher, more spiritual level of the individual. Romans 12:2 says it like this: "And be not conformed to this world: but be ye transformed by the renewing of your mind, that ye may

prove what is that good, and acceptable, and perfect, will of God."
We of the Western world have come to rely so heavily on the conscious mind that we have lost the awareness that our lives can be
greatly transformed by the unconscious. In recent years, however,
the Western world has shown a rebirth of interest in dreams and an
understanding that they can be valuable tools for objective, practical
guidance, as well as for subjective insights and spiritual-physical-
mental directives. If we learn to interpret them properly, and then to
apply what we have learned, they can be a powerful instrument for
personal growth. Dreams can give us guidance to physical healing,
making money, career opportunities, and a host of other areas important in our everyday life.

The intent and purpose of this book is to stimulate and encourage
working with your dreams. We believe such a reference manual can
be most helpful when you first start to record, work with, and interpret your dreams. It is our hope that, as a guide to self-analysis
through dream interpretation, it will aid in establishing good habits
for the person on the path of self-improvement.

WHAT IS A SYMBOL?

Approximately one thousand symbols which commonly occur in
dreams are listed. Webster's dictionary says a symbol is a token,
pledge, or sign by which one infers a thing; something that stands for
or represents another thing; an object used to represent an abstrac-
tion. The dove is a symbol of peace. The cross represents the crucify-
ing of the lower nature of humans at the thyroid level, to their higher,
spiritual nature. (See Archetypes chapter for the significance of the
endocrine system.) This is just the beginning of how a symbol works.

Let's look briefly at some of the common types of symbols. The
conventional symbol is one that is accepted and agreed upon by a large
group of people—flags, words, totem poles, saris, clan plaids, to
name a few. The *accidental symbol*, in contrast, is an individual symbol
(a specific person, for instance) and is the most important in dream
interpretation. It is usually not meaningful to anyone but the
dreamer. Accidental symbols may be anything, but they are usually
people. You may have an aunt or an uncle who is very meaningful to
you because he/she is very loving and kind. When this person is
present in a dream, your dream may be telling you that, like this
person, you have been loving and kind to someone that day or
should be loving and kind in the situation brought up by the dream.
You may know someone who talks too much, in fact may be con-

sidered a gossip. When such a person turns up in a dream, your dream may be saying that you have talked too much or gossiped that day.

Another kind of symbol is the *universal*, or the *Archetype*. Carl Jung travelled the world over to prove his suspicion that all people share certain symbols and that they mean the same thing to everyone. Removed from all other society, thousands of miles apart and with no means of communication, people in the African jungles used symbols with meanings identical to other peoples'. There is something deep within the subconscious that causes us all to react in the same way to these symbols though we are not consciously aware of their meaning. Examples are the crescent, square, triangle, circle, some fairy tales, to name a few.

It is difficult to convert the riddles, images, and metaphors of the subconscious, unlimited mind to the verbal language of the conscious, reasoning mind. One problem is that people often use language to deceive and to manipulate things for their own benefit. In dreams alone, one can return to one's original, unlimited mind, the mind one had in the Garden of Eden before the fall. A significant dream can be worked on for a long period of time, with different meanings emerging as the dreamer attempts to probe the psychic depths of symbols in the conscious, waking state. The dream source is honest, but we, though rational beings, are not always honest. To gain in self awareness we must work to become more honest about ourselves. The obscurity in dreams may actually help soul development in that it prevents deceit between the conscious and the subconscious levels of the mind. For instance, we may not want to admit consciously that we eat too much, drink too much, smoke too much, talk too much, indulge negative thoughts or attitudes. The subconscious subtly nudges us onto a more disciplined path through obscure symbols, because the conscious mind may be unable to handle a direct message.

Not having use of verbal language, the subconscious mind must gain access to the conscious mind through the use of images to metaphorically convey a message. Abstracts such as moods, feelings, responses are especially difficult to express metaphorically. Also, non-linguistic symbols do not have the exactitude or clarity of linguistic symbols—at least not to the conscious mind, which has the task of "decoding" the message. Another reason for the ambiguity of some symbols is that the very clever subconscious mind may combine in one image an event currently experienced with similar past experiences. Some symbols may be indecipherable. In that case, simply put the dream aside until the message is presented again, using a more recognizable image.

The word "Truth" is used many times and is explained in the glossary of terms at the end of the book. Scripture says, "Ye shall know the Truth and the Truth shall set you free." A dream, properly interpreted, will give the feeling of freedom, such as might come from freeing yourself of an old guilt feeling.

"Reading" is a term used to describe the clairvoyant discourses which Edgar Cayce gave while in a self-induced hypnotic sleep-state. Over 15,000 stenographic transcripts of these psychic statements, covering a forty-five year period, are in the custody of the Edgar Cayce Foundation, Virginia Beach, Virginia. The Cayce readings constitute one of the largest, most impressive records of psychic perception ever to emanate from a single individual. These readings include the subjects of medicine and health, past and present incarnations, business, dream interpretation, mental and spiritual states, home, marriage, and almost nine hundred miscellaneous subjects.

While in this self-induced sleep-state, the mind of Edgar Cayce seemed capable of transcending time and space, tapping the collective unconscious minds of all people, past, present, and in some cases apparently the future. When given a subject's name and location, followed by a suggestion, he would proceed to describe that person, the individual's body, physical condition or illnesses, mental and emotional states, and what was causing any problem. Cayce would then prescribe remedies, among them physical therapy, surgery, medicine, diet, exercise, and even psychological guidance. This talent for medical diagnosis was demonstrated repeatedly for many years although Cayce himself had no medical background nor technical education in any related field.

In 1931 the Association for Research and Enlightenment (A.R.E.) was established as a non-profit educational organization, to preserve, study, and present the Cayce clairvoyant readings. This open membership association continues to research the readings and promote lectures, seminars, conferences, and study groups. We are both members of the A.R.E. field team in the Greater Kansas City area of Kansas and Missouri. Our special interests have been dreams and meditation, both subjects steeped with symbols. For more than twelve years we have worked with many people in weekly dream study groups, where they have brought their recorded dreams of the previous week and, in round-table fashion, each person has related what the dream means to him or her. Much of our source material comes from them.

Though this collection was originally intended for our personal use, we realized it would be useful to anyone interested in dreams and their meaning. As the bibliography will indicate, we have done a vast amount of research and have also attended many symposiums on dreams in Kansas City and at the A.R.E. headquarters at Virginia Beach. We are striving to offer a service to the widest possible audience, and one that can be used by the professional as well as the novice. We hope this work will serve to expand the thinking and the imagination of our readers, and to assist them in their goal of greater self-awareness. When working with your dreams, use this manual as a springboard. Perhaps it will be the answer to your dreams.

The Dream Dictionary

1

Getting to Know Our Dreams

RECALLING DREAMS

The first step in working with dreams is remembering them. Some people, because of poor recall, claim that they don't dream. However, dream research has shown that virtually everyone has four or five dreams per night, at approximately ninety-minute intervals. Non-recall can have many causes—illness, fatigue, medications, drugs, disinterest, repression (the dreamer must be willing to change). The Edgar Cayce readings say that people who don't remember their dreams are not so close to the spiritual life as they should be.

Anyone who wishes to improve dream recall should consider the following suggestions:

- Think about dreams, talk about dreams, read about dreams. In other words, allow your dream life to become an important part of your waking life. Join a dream study group or start one within the family structure. Senoi Indians, as well as Mayans, believe that by just listening to the dreams of their children something therapeutic takes place; they had no crimes of violence within their communities as long as they followed this practice. At breakfast all children under twelve years of age are encouraged to talk about the dreams of the previous night.

- Before going to sleep, mentally review your feelings, activities, responses, physical conditions of that day. (Don't expect dreams to be an oracle: conscious efforts toward an answer to a question must come first.) Then, get a full night's sleep, awakening naturally, if possible.

- Be open to change, and willing to accept the meaning of the dream even if it threatens present beliefs or attitudes.

- Keep a dream journal. A special notebook, pencil and a light, flashlight if necessary, must be near your bed and not just "for show"; convincing the subconscious of your sincerity in this project (thereby securing its cooperation) is vital. Record your dream immediately upon awakening; otherwise the dream will distort and you may miss an important symbol. If a dream is recalled upon awakening during the night, write down a phrase or key word that will trigger a full recall in the morning. Mentally reviewing a dream at this point, and then going back to sleep, just doesn't work for recall—most dreams will be lost. You must write down something—a fragment, symbol, action, name, person, scene, feeling. Record the dream in the present tense (present tense conveys the feeling of relevancy better than the past tense). If a dream is recalled during the day, write it down, along with what was happening at the moment of recall.

- Use pre-sleep suggestion, and pray. (Repeat "I *will* remember my dreams upon awakening.")

Once you have learned to recall dreams with some degree of regularity (two or three a week), you may want to try incubating a dream. Dream incubation is consciously generating a dream to help solve a problem, make a decision, heal a relationship, overcome self-defeating attitudes or habits. There are several useful steps you may follow.

- Spend fifteen or twenty minutes just before bedtime writing in detail about the problem.

- Form a question concerning the problem. ("What attitudes or responses can I change to bring about a better relationship with John?") Focus your mind on the question while drifting off to sleep.

- Upon awakening, record any dream memories—people (known or unknown), situations, feelings, impressions, fragments.

Impressive anecdotal evidence indicates that group dream incubation can be very rewarding. The only requirements are that each member have a common interest in dreams and that they follow the same procedure. It is suggested that they drink nothing alcoholic before going to bed and that a period of Bible reading and prayer and meditation be observed, asking for a dream to help the designated target person. It is not necessary that members of this group know each other, or the problem their dreams are being asked to help solve, in fact it is better if they don't. The following morning, members of this group report their dreams to the target person. The results can be profound; you indeed become aware that in some way we are all connected. For more detailed information on dream recall, dream incubation, or dream interpretation, we recommend *How to Interpret Your Dreams* by Mark Thurston, available from A.R.E., Virginia Beach, Virginia 23451.

TYPES OF DREAMS

There are within the flesh body three levels—physical, mental, spiritual—each providing a particular type of dream. We use these broad categories only as a convenience for description and as an interpretative aid. Keep in mind that many dreams can be interpreted on more than one level, and also that there is much overlapping of types. For example, a compensatory dream may also be a wish-fulfillment dream. Which of the three levels initiates the dream is not important. The primary consideration in our life is how we use the information obtained: the real interpretation of a dream is in the application of what is learned.

Physical

Dreams originating from the physical level are the easiest to identify and understand. Some are meaningful, showing a physiological need, such as exercise, balanced diet, medical care, sexual release, meditation. Others are meaningless, often simply responses to external stimuli, for example a bad food combination, overindulgence in food or drink, a drug, hormonal imbalance, bodily injury or illness, or any intrusion on the physical senses (such as a bright light, a cold draft, a pungent odor). A common dream experience is substituting the ringing of a telephone for a real-life alarm clock, or dreaming of a snow storm and awakening to a realization that the physical body is cold. Drugs, overindulgence in food or drink, hard to digest foods, or a harried life style can produce meaningless dreams in another way—they may distort the information.

Everyday activities sometimes trigger meaningless dreams. We call them "hodge-podge" dreams—a rehash of what has been going on. After spending a rainy day entertaining her four small children, a mother dreamed of climbing a mountain of broken Crayolas. A salesman, driving several hours at night, dreamed of a continuous stream of headlights coming toward him. These are examples of a carry-over from the day's activities and probably do not warrant further interpretation. However, don't be too hasty in labeling a dream "physical"—an important message from another level may be missed.

Mental

The largest number of dreams is initiated by the subconscious, the mental level. Dreams from this level are more complicated and cover a wider area of experience. Many of these dreams can be a valuable tool for guidance or problem solving. One dreamer was mulling over whether to pursue a particular relationship. This matter was on her mind one night when she had the following dream: "I am in a field digging potatoes, but they are too hot to handle." What could be more clear? This is an interestng example of how clichés may be used in dreams to make a point: "Drop it like a hot potato!"

Of course, you can always ignore the guidance offered by the dream, but to know that "someone up there cares" can also be a matter of great importance to you. A woman who had worked for some time on a self-improvement discipline for better control of her emotions (adrenals) was beginning to feel it was hopeless when she had this dream: she was in her brother Dan's apartment, on the bed with a lion (the archetypal symbol for the adrenals). It was purring and snuggling up to her like a kitten; she had complete control over it. Since her brother didn't share her enthusiasm about dreams, she associated the Dan of her dream with Daniel in the Lion's den and his ability to control the lions (here, a symbol of her emotions). She was greatly encouraged. A horse-racing enthusiast dreamed of going to the track and finding it dusty and overgrown with weeds. Later he wished he had "listened" to the dream, because he did, indeed, go through a "dry spell" at the race track.

Contrary to the expectations of many dreamers, our nightly guru does not tell us what to do, but gives us useful information which we are free to accept or reject. A food-loving dreamer had a repetitive dream of being so obese that he could neither walk nor sit, just stand around. The dream does not say "stop overeating," but it certainly paints a vivid picture of the direction he is going. Another dream also demonstrates how we are given information, leaving the application of the message up to the dreamer: "My year-old grand-daughter can detach her head from her body, her little round head tearing around the house. I tell my daughter that she should teach her baby not to do that because the head is too hard to catch." The dreamer discussed the dream with her daughter, and they decided to watch for signs of an overly headstrong disposition in the baby.

Because many of our problems derive from a lack of inner awareness, the self-revealing dream is closely related to the problem-solving dream. Do not be afraid of what these dreams may reveal. As Carl Jung put it, "It is of first importance for the assimilation of dream-contents that no violence be done to the real values of the conscious personality." In other words, we will not be given more than we are able to deal with at the time. Invaluable insights can be gained through these dreams. One woman, wondering how to improve a relationship, received the following dream message: "There is a small growth on the side of my tongue. I look in the mirror and see that I am growing an additional tongue." Subsequently, she conscientiously "watched her tongue" and the relationship improved. Another dream concerning speech had the dreamer being chased by an alligator (known for its destructive mouth). Obviously, the speech of the second dreamer was more vicious than the first dreamer's.

Some dream messages are more obscure: "I watch as two men pour gasoline on two kittens and set them afire." Don't waste energy (gas) even on small or trivial gossip ("cattiness")—it can be inflammatory. The two men and kittens may symbolize the duality of gossip (listening/repeating). Happily, some self-awareness dreams are positive: "My hair is set in rollers for a permanent, ready to be saturated with lamb broth." The dreamer took it to mean that the thinking (hair) is all "set" and ready to be permeated with the spirit of the Lamb (Jesus). If most dreams seem to be negative, don't be discouraged. Remember, they usually come to assist with a problem, or point out a deficiency, or correct us when we err. Our dispenser of night visions apparently does not believe it is necessary to give too many "pats on the back," but when it does give one, there will be no mistaking the meaning, for they are usually beautiful dreams from which you wake with a feeling of contentment.

Here is an example of how self-awareness can help solve problems. This dream came to a woman who felt her husband always belittled her and did not appreciate her contributions to home and business: "I am walking in the woods and come across a cave. Out of the cave come two small spotted leopards, growling at me. I attack them bare-handed. One I throw over my shoulder into the woods;

the other I kill and drag home to show my husband. 'Look at this leopard I just killed bare-handed,' I say. His reply is, 'That's no leopard: You just killed a big cat.' I look at the leopard and see that the spots are gone. It does look like a big cat." The dreamer is in a state of confusion (woods) over this problem (leopards) and wonders how to handle it. She is shown two ways: She can throw the problem (her feelings of being unappreciated) away, back into its confused state, or she can grapple with it and drag it back to her house (look at it consciously). Once she decides to handle the problem out in the open rather than keep it buried in the subconscious (the cave), then she can change her response to her husband's put-downs (the leopard *did* change its spots). Now her problem is a "pussy cat" and not a wild animal (uncontrolled emotions). We did not feel that in this dream bringing the problem "out in the open" meant confronting her husband, but rather her own disquietude. Most of the time our efforts to "change the spots" on someone else are ineffective. Our dreams come to help us change our own "spots."

Another example of self-awareness through dreams comes from a man who had a recurring dream of walking around like a zombie, totally unconcerned with what was going on around him. After he realized that the message was to be more emotionally responsive, and followed the advice, the dream stopped.

The content of some dreams is so anxiety-laden, or even terrifying, that we are awakened, often with a pounding heart and sweaty palms. Most people occasionally experience nightmares. They may be a warning, literal or symbolic; they may be expressing a fear that needs overcoming; a few may be a preparation, rehearsing emotions under stress so that their real-life occurrence will be easier. Whatever their purpose, nightmares demand our attention. Most dreamers would rather ignore them because of the terrifying content, but they come to help remind us of a problem that we are not handling. The message may have been presented many times before in a benign way but not remembered or dealt with. We should remember, too, that dreams may exaggerate, sometimes a great deal, depending on the personality of the dreamer. Dreamers soon learn through experience and dream-work if they have highly exaggerated dreams. Repetitive nightmares are particularly important, stemming from an overwhelming problem or emotional conflict repressed during waking life.

Here are a few common anxiety dreams with some symbolical meanings: *falling*—losing control; feeling helpless; falling from grace; sexual guilt ("fallen" woman); having no support or foundation; losing status; fear of failure; *drowning*—overwhelming emotion or warning of pneumonia (fluid in lungs); being "over your head" in something; feeling helpless; *being chased*—trying to escape someone or something; fear of getting "caught," of something that is going to "catch up with you"; not wanting to face something; *being unable to speak or call out*—fear of inadequately or improperly expressing oneself; feeling defenseless; *paralysis*—making no progress; debilitating illness; feeling impotent, useless; can be a diet dream where not being able to move symbolizes constipation.

We should always pay close attention to stressful dreams in which the physical body is in difficulty. Our subconscious has the ability to sense an illness and to send a dream warning long before symptoms appear. Dreams of breathing difficulties might be warnings of a lung disease; constrictions around the chest area may indicate heart disease. Occasional nightmares are probably caused by mere passing concerns; however, recurring nightmares that have a common theme should be scrutinized for hints of possible mental or physical illness. This allows for early detection at a treatable stage.

It is vital to bring the nightmare to a peaceful conclusion, either through lucid dreaming or through a waking reverie, or daydream. Many persons have dream experiences similar to this one: "I am being chased by two ferocious dogs. I say to myself, 'Hey, wait a minute! This is my dream, and I can change these dogs into friendly ones.' I turn and face a big shaggy dog, wagging its tail." This is an example of *lucid dreaming*—being aware of dreaming while in the dream state. The dreamer can control and guide the dream activities and images. This way of dreaming is especially advantageous in overcoming fears. It is a form of clairvoyance. For instance, if the dreamer is fleeing from an ominous figure, he or she should turn and face the pursuer, meeting the threat head-on and overcoming it (enlisting the aid of other dream images, if necessary). Or, preferably, the dreamer can face the enemy, find out what it wants, and transform it into a friendly, helpful image. If the dreamer is unsuccessful in establishing a lucid dream state, then he or she should recreate the dream through reverie or day-dreaming, and by the same procedure change its outcome. What is taking place at the subconscious level will eventually become a conscious fact, and we can learn to change our fears into conquests.

Every conscious act, attitude, or emotion that goes too far will inevitably call for a subconscious *compensatory readjustment*, a self-regulating system that maintains a necessary balance in the psyche. This self-regulation often comes through dreams. For instance, a dream of laughing a lot may be compensating for an attitude that is too serious. It may be saying don't take things so seriously, have more fun! One woman, having a difficult time adjusting to a totally new environment and area of the country, felt serious about everything in her life. She no longer had the security of family and long-time friends who she knew accepted her as she is. She had this dream: she was lying on a day-bed nude (exposed and relaxed), when an old school friend appeared with whom she associated a good sense of humor. She got the message. From that day on, each time she felt inadequate in her new environment, she thought about this dream; she relaxed and looked for the humor in her own attitude of worry and concern. Hers was, clearly, a very helpful dream in read-justment. Conversely, a dream of crying a lot may be saying that something needs to be taken more seriously. Calorie-counters fre-quently have dreams of eating "forbidden" food; people who need to lose weight will often have recurring dreams of pushing full carts through food stores, as if to say that food is a big part of their life. Carl Jung advises that in interpreting any dream it is always helpful to ask for what conscious act or attitude it compensates.

Closely associated with the compensatory dream is the *wish-fulfillment* dream. Finding money or valuables in a dream may reflect a wish to be relieved of a tight economic situation. A shy person may dream of giving a brilliant speech in front of the United Nations. A person without a love life may be walking down the street with an unknown person who has their arms around them and is very loving. But don't be too quick to categorize a dream as merely wish-fulfillment. Such dreams may be telling the dreamer where he can "find" money, or be encouraging the dreamer to speak up, people want to hear what he has to say. Look for the other levels of dream interpretation until you find the one that fits. Often all levels will apply.

Some dreams defy a rational explanation, at least at this stage of dream knowledge. These are popularly called ESP dreams and in-volve telepathy, clairvoyance, or precognition. The Bible abounds with prophetic dreams. There are many authenticated reports of indi-viduals who dreamed of a loved one when in distress or at the time of their death. Hitler, while on the front in World War I, claimed to have had a dream in which he saw himself buried by earth and molten iron. Upon awakening, he left his position. Moments later the spot where he had been was the target of an explosion, burying his com-panions under an avalanche of earth. Abraham Lincoln's dream of seeing his coffin just a few days before he died is a well-known prophetic dream.

From our own files is the following, which the dreamer had many times: "I am living with my in-laws in a big, old-fashioned house. I discover a hidden room which no one else knows about. It is beauti-fully appointed with red velvet draperies and a grand piano in the center of the room." In time the dreamer moved to California and visited a New Age church. And there she found her "hidden room" with red velvet draperies and a grand piano just as her dream had pictured. The metaphysical philosophy of the church became a great source of inspiration and contentment. She felt that the setting of the dream—her in-law's house—was very appropriate because they were not open to metaphysical teachings. Hence, this particular approach to spirituality would be unknown to them in their state of consciousness (their house).

Most repetitive, or recurring dreams deal with some unresolved issue. Though often reflecting fears that need to be overcome, the dream may be urging the dreamer to look at something differently. Climbing a mountain that seems endlessly steep and arduous may be about a goal the dreamer has in sight, which should be reassessed. Perhaps it is not really worth the effort.

Not infrequently a dream provides a convenient escape valve, a way of letting off steam that would be unacceptable in waking life. A dream of verbally or physically attacking an overbearing boss could be a safe release for a person with repressed hostile feelings. This is a better way to handle aggressive emotions than keeping them bottled up, affecting physical and mental health.

Spiritual

Of all our dreams, those emanating from the spiritual level have the greatest transformative effect. Once recalled, they are seldom forgotten. They leave us with a feeling of wholeness and harmony. They encourage, inspire, and give insights into the meaning of life. Sometimes a religious figure of importance to the dreamer appears, advising or enlightening. Other symbols also may suggest a spiritual theme: a mountain top, light (natural or artificial), High Self figures (see Dream Characters chapter), a rainbow, celestial objects, angels, religious articles, any body of water, especially clear water, any euphoric feeling. Hearing one's name called may be the superconscious calling one to greater spiritual service; a knocking may be the Christ-spirit knocking, waiting to be received. Even if the manifest dream content is forgotten, the feeling of confidence, peace, and wholeness remains. Remember, though, if we want to have beautiful, inspiring, uplifting dreams, we must do our best to encourage those qualities in our daily lives.

Here is a dream that came to support and encourage someone in a spiritual quest: "I am standing by a stream of water, feeling alone, as if I am the only person in the world. I kneel down to clean a fish with a stone and see a figure in a long, rose-colored garment standing beside me. It is Jesus." The metaphysical influences in this dreamer's life ("stream of life") were foreign to her background and to her environment (feeling alone). She is putting the finishing touches on her spirituality (cleaning the fish) with knowledge (stone). Jesus' appearance reassures her that she is never alone and that His love (rose-colored robe) will always sustain her. This dream of great comfort helped her determination to pursue metaphysical studies.

Some dreams may be actual scenes or memories from a past life. Closely examine any dream that seems to be in a different time period with different environs and dress. It may classify as a past-life dream. Edgar Cayce said that past-life dreams come not only to assist in resolving present-day conflicts, but to help awaken the spiritual core of the dreamer. In the Cayce files is a dream in which a young man saw himself in an ancient warrior's outfit with a sword in his hand. Cayce confirmed that this was a dream of a past life and that the dreamer was now to use the old fierceness of his warrior-self to keep him patient and resolute in serving others.

WORKING WITH DREAMS

The first approach to dream interpretation is to determine whether the dream will lend itself to a literal interpretation. If so, then take the appropriate action in real life. In a dream, one woman was informed at a service station that the oil level in her car was low. The next day this alert dreamer checked and found that it was indeed dangerously low. Don't assume, however, that the literal message is the only message: dreams often have more than one level of meaning. Another dreamer pictured herself driving up a hill, getting stalled, and backing down. This dream came during a busy Christmas season, and the dreamer wisely decided it was saying that she didn't have enough energy to "make the grade" and she should literally "back down." Two days later she tried to start her car and found the battery dead. This is a dream that may have two levels of meaning—one literal, and one for the physical body. Skillfully skating on ice in a dream may be saying, "You're performing well in a cold, potentially dangerous situation." On the other hand, skating well on ice is known as figure skating, so the dream may be suggesting that the dreamer "work on his figure." It may also be pointing out a latent talent. Most dreams that seem to be literal statements, about a death or catastrophic illness, for example, mean that something in the dreamer's life is dying, such as a relationship or interest in a project.

Don't overlook word-play in analyzing dreams. The pun, cliché, double entendre, colloquialism—all add sparkle and wit to many dreams. Searching for the double meaning also tests the creativity of the conscious mind. A young woman dreamed that all the farm animals left the farms and ran amuck. She missed the word-play, and it was only weeks later, when she and her husband separated, that the meaning became clear: her domestic life (farm animals) had indeed "run amuck." Another dreamer was entertaining a lot of people in her home: in real-life she was "entertaining" a lot of different ideas in her conscious mind (her home). Yet another dream involved a hippopotamus being kept in a fireplace. The dreamer laughingly admitted that for her problem hips she needed to burn up some calories. Another example of a punning message: "I have a bump on the side of my nose. On closer examination I discover that it is another nose." This dreamer had two choices of interpretation—she was either being "too nosey" about something, or she needed to be "nosier." (Only the dreamer knows what is relevant to make the accurate interpretation.) One man was puzzled by a mantel that appeared in several dreams. The mystery unraveled when he thought of "mantle" and finally "cloak." (He was trying to hide something that needed to be brought out in the open.) The symbol did not reappear. A nickel may stand for the five senses (five cents); altar may mean alter; guilt may be represented by gilt; a swing may point to a type of person (a "swinger"); a veil may substitute for "to veil" (conceal). The list is endless.

Sometimes a cliché summarizes the entire meaning of a dream. A speeding train that crashes into an oncoming train may be a warning: be careful, you're "on the wrong track"! Another example: "I am driving very fast in my new car. The car goes out of control on a curve, plunging into a body of water." A likely interpretation: slow down before you end up "in the drink," or "over your head," or "in deep water." Whichever stereotyped phrase is selected, the message is clear.

If neither the literal interpretation seems applicable, nor the message concealed in word-play, we suggest following these steps:

(1) Review the types of dreams. Can the dream be tagged to one of them?

(2) Try to guess what the dream is about. Dreams are usually concerned with current problems and interests, and we don't have to dig very far to find the association. They rarely comment on issues in which the dreamer has little or no involvement.

(3) Re-experience the emotions in the dream. Do they relate to present conditions or relationships?

(4) Identify the setting. This helps determine what area of one's life is being addressed. Is the locale inside or outside? Familiar or unfamiliar? Daytime or nighttime? A specific season of the year? Spring may indicate a time of new growth, a new beginning; summer, a time to harvest what has been sown; autumn, a time to gather and store "seeds" for an inactive, restful phase; winter, a time to nurture growth that is waiting to burst forth and initiate a new cycle of productivity. Winter may also denote a "frozen," nonproductive stage. Again, the dreamer knows which interpretation is relevant. As Hugh Lynn Cayce put it, "Interpret the dreamer and not the dream."

(5) Extract the basic theme of the dream, limiting it to a one-sentence summation, like an advertisement for a movie. If the dream is long, with changing scenes, write a theme for each section, emphasizing the actions rather than the actors. If we had to pick one way of working with a dream, this would be it. Here is a sample dream: "I am driving down a road. A car in front of me goes off the road and is sinking in a body of water. I get out of my car and call, 'Can I help you?' The driver, an Oriental, looks at me angrily and shakes his fist. I am perplexed because I can see that he needs help." *Theme:* Someone needs help, but refuses it.

Notice that no attempt is made to analyze the actions or symbols. That comes later. At this point the meaning of the dream may be clear and further investigation unnecessary. However, if the dreamer feels that more information can be uncovered, continue with the next step.

(6) Analyze the symbols. After establishing the context in which the symbol appears (developed in steps 3, 4, and 5), isolate each dream character and examine the role he plays in real life. (See Dream Characters chapter.) Next, look at each object. What is it? What does it do? How does it work? What is it used for? The dreamer's understanding and ideas are what is important here, not objective accuracy. Does it trigger a remembrance of something or someone? What are the personal associations, if any? Amplification of this kind may help pinpoint the issue.

Referring to the alphabetized words for ideas can help, but we make the point that *the meanings listed are suggestions, not*

dogmatic definitions. Even archetypes must give way to the subjective association. For instance, a bull is often an archetypal
symbol for the sexual urge. But one man's dream which included a bull—not once, but twice in the same dream—made
sense to him only after he related it to the "bullish" market at
that time. The ups and downs of Wall Street were important to
him, and an inflexible approach to dream-symbol interpretation would have obscured some practical guidance.

(7) Arrive at a preliminary interpretation. The dreamer is now
ready to make an intellectual interpretation. But the final interpretation is revealed in the next, and last, step.

(8) Apply what has been learned. The emphasis on application is
one of the unique characteristics of the Cayce readings approach to dream work. They tell us that as we apply day by
day what we know, "then is the next step, the next act, the
next experience, shown thee." This is also true for our dream
life. The goal of the dream is to guide us in altering our behavior, attitudes, and emotions, to aid us in transforming the
lower, materialistic nature into the higher, spiritualistic nature. As we work towards a practical application of the dream
message, as we understand it, deeper levels of meaning will
unfold.

The interpretation of a dream may be easier if, by putting two or
three dreams together, we look for a common feature. Examine a
number of dreams and see if a pattern emerges, or a common thread,
revealing a preoccupation. Sometimes a series shows a progression of
ideas; sometimes it shows alternatives, different ways of working
through a problem until a solution is found; sometimes it shows more
aspects of a situation, making it clearer. For instance, dream number
two may add something not revealed, or overlooked, in dream number one; dream number three may add more information or correct a
misinterpretation.

Don't be afraid of making a "wrong" interpretation. Fortunately,
dreams are self-correcting: if you have misinterpreted one dream, a
simpler one will get the message through. After most dreams that
refuse to reveal their secrets, less obscure dreams follow. All dreams
are understood at the deeper levels of consciousness. For those who
study their dreams and apply what they learn, it isn't necessary to
comprehend everything in order to benefit from the unlimited perspective of the dream. Even forgotten dreams may aid people who
conscientiously and sincerely try to create a cooperative, friendly relationship with their subconscious.

2

An Alphabet of Common Symbols

· A ·

ABDOMEN · belly, the place of feelings, emotions; the place where you express either courage or cowardice. Can convert hostile feelings to love. "No guts"; "the gut feeling." (See *stomach*)

ABORTION · not allowing the full development of something new and precious in an attitude or emotion. Cutting off the life flow.

ABSENCE · (See Dream Characters chapter)

ABSURDITIES · when senseless, ridiculous matters show up in a dream, they may be reminding you that all is of one force.

ACCIDENT · usually a warning of some kind, making a wreck of life or things.

AIR · element associated with the fourth spiritual center, the thymus; mental activity. *Turbulent air—an overwrought mind. "Breath of life." (See tornado, hurricane, etc.)*

ALARM · alarm clock ringing, fire alarm, sirens, etc., a warning; or wake up and live.

ALCOHOL · spirits, impediment to spiritual growth; can be related to diet (too much sugar creates alcohol in the system).

ALLEY · if it is dark and sinister, the dreamer may feel he or she has strayed into an unpleasant situation. If it comes to a dead end, the dream could indicate a feeling of being in a situation which has no way out. The back way—taking short cuts. "Alley cat"; "right up his alley."

ALTAR/ALTER · worship, sacrifice; the altar in a dream may be showing the dreamer what he worships, depending on what is there. Consider the play on words—does something need to be altered in your life?

ANDROGYNOUS · (See Archetypes chapter)

ANGER · temper, almost always the dreamer's; may be a warning to control your temper.

ANTIQUES · old traits or values; if they are beautiful, it could mean potential; genuine origin, time-honored; sound, proved authority; possible karmic tie; classical, simple beauty, artistic; ageless wisdom. "That's an antique."

APPEARANCE · in dreams, the appearance is important. The expression—smiling, frowning, etc.—tells what emotion the person is trying to get across. Appearance may also call attention to a particular part—*arms* usually represent service since they are used for carrying burdens. Question then what is in your arms or on them. *Bloated appearance*—ill health, egotism, debility, excessive burdens. *Tired expressions, distortion of eyes, ears, nose, chin or mouth*—warning of distortion in those areas. *Eyes*—awareness. *Nose*—nose trouble, "nosey"; "don't bite your nose off to spite your face." *Ears*—hearing, "hear no evil"; "now hear this"; are you listening?"; "lend me your ears." *Chin* or *mouth* has to do with speech; to "take it on the chin"; "mouth off." A closed mouth may be saying keep your mouth shut. *Legs, calf, or thigh*—what carries you on your path (mental, physical, or spiritual). *Feet*—understanding (they are under your standing). (Check for the literal, physical meaning of the appearance.)

APPLAUSE · encouragement and approval; if negative symbols appear, it could indicate egotism.

APPLES · could represent temptation, as in the Garden of Eden; also signifies sexual knowledge. "An apple a day"; "apple of your eye"; "apple pie order"; "one rotten apple spoils the whole barrel." (See *food*)

ARCHAEOLOGY · dig within yourself for answers; buried values from the past. Could be from another lifetime.

ARGUMENT · warning of emotional tensions that may get out of hand; warning about arguing with conscience or others; sign of moral or mental conflicts within.

ARK · *rainbow*—God's promise of no more floods to destroy the earth. *Ark of the covenant*—Israel's eternal relationship with the creator. *Noah's Ark*—preservation of man's animal instincts while on earth.

ARMS · (See *appearance*)

ARROW · vengeance; unpleasant news; message coming (arrows were used in early times to carry messages); love (Cupid's arrow through the heart).

ART · values on display; ideals "hung-up," need for putting them into practice. (See *diorama*)

ATTIC · storehouse of the conscious mind. (See *house*)

AUTOMOBILE · (See Vehicles chapter)

AUTUMN · (See *seasons*)

· B ·

BACK · physical strength, endurance, bearer of burdens. *Backbone*—firmness, decisiveness, ability to stand in face of opposition; power to endure without being overcome. *Backward movement*—going backward in life.

BAPTISM · a new beginning; rededication required or an increase of the Holy Spirit; renewal through a washing away of the old state.

BARE · (See *naked*)

BAREFOOT · a socially inappropriate appearance in many public places, therefore, insensitive to conformity when appearing barefooted in conventional areas. *Tenderfooted*—true understanding (under standing).

BATHING · cleansing mentally, physically, or spiritually; may be saying that this is what you need to do.

BATTLEFIELD · impulses at war with each other; hostile and aggressive attitudes.

BEACH · relaxation and pleasure. "To be beached."

BELLS · communication; reminder of something; the dreamer's conscience; *Ship bells*—tell time: it's later than you think. *Church bells*—a call to worship. "Saved by the bell" (as in a fight); "with bells on" (eager).

BIBLE · God's laws. As the Edgar Cayce readings often quote from the Bible, "study to show thyself worthy."

BIRTH · same symbol as babies—giving birth to new, higher ideals; wish fullfillment (desire to be a more complete woman). (See *seed*)

BITING · to be annoyed or upset, to wound or be wounded. Your hand in the mouth of an animal (an animal taking you by the hand) may be a positive or negative indication; for example, a dreamer may be told his or her stubborness is excessive by a dream of having a hand between the teeth of one or more stubborn animals, such as a mule or camel; this leaves an imprint. On the positive side, sheep are known for meekness. If the bite draws blood, the meaning is intensified, as in the symbol of losing the life flow. When the negative animal appears, especially two of them, there is a strong need to work on correcting the trait they represent.

BITTER · bitter drink; aversion, abhorrence, humiliation.

BLANKET · comfort, rest, protection, red blanket in a hospital means critical case. "Blanket of stars"; "blanket of snow."

BLINDNESS · being blind to certain facts; groping around in the darkness of confusion and ignorance; not facing reality. "Blind spot"; "blind as a bat."

BLOOD · the dream with blood in it is usually a dream with a powerful message, it usually represents the loss of the life flow. *Dark Red*—negative emotions; loss of vital energy. *Menstrual blood*—an awakening to life's creative power; related to internal cleansing. "To get your blood up" (be enraged); "blood on your hands"; "in cold blood."

BOOTS · "These boots were made for walking." To "boot" someone or something out (to get rid of). (See *shoes*)

BRAIN · gray matter; the area for thinking; convoluted spinal column (See *thirty-three* in Numbers chapter); intellectual power. "To pick someone's brains"; "to beat your brains out"; "a brain is only as strong as its weakest think." (See *hats, caps, hair*)

BREAD · inner substance; the "staff of life." To "break bread'; "Man does not live by bread alone"; "Bread of life" (Christ); "bread" (money). (See *mana*)

· C ·

CAGE · imprisonment; restraint of some ordinarily free spirit or impulse; needs restrained; entrapped. Seeing an animal in a cage may symbolize the dreamer's own pent-up impulses or emotions; could be saying to set something free. "Caged in."

CAMPING · temporary measures; getting next to nature. Someone or something is "camping on your doorstep."

CANCER · fourth sign of the Zodiac; growth in a negative way; something that eats away at the dreamer.

CANDLE · spiritual light. Refer to Spiritual Centers section for meaning of number of candles in dream. "Doesn't hold a candle to" (inferior); "burning the candle at both ends."

CANDY · could be a warning, since sugar and starches produce a kind of alcohol. "Easy as taking candy from a baby."

CANNIBALISM · something forbidden; someone is living off someone else.

CANYON · long, intensive experience from which there is no easy escape, and through which there is a flowing stream of emotion, as water may flow through the floor of a canyon.

CAPS · thoughts; head. "Set your cap for"; "thinking cap"; "graduation cap"; "cap in hand" (humility); "caps" (capital letter emphasis; also a noise-making device.) (See *brain, hats*)

CAR · (See Vehicles chapter)

CARD · could be a death symbol, especially if it is a spade; hearts, diamonds, clubs—look for play on words. "He's a card"; "it's in the cards"; "play your cards right."

CARPET · covering up something; being walked on. (Pay attention to the colors)

CARRIAGE · (See Vehicles chapter)

CAROUSEL · going around in circles. (See *merry-go-round*)

CARVING(S) · *carving meat*—hostility, aggression. *Carving one's initials* (or design) on wood or other surfaces—the desire to leave an imprint on something. *Carving a statue* or other object—confidence in, or desire for artistic ability; patterns of thought and behavior.

CATASTROPHES · the demand for a change of attitude. These may come in the form of explosions, bombs, earthquakes, floods, etc.

CEMETERIES · death fears or wishes; thoughts about someone who is dead, or what is dead and buried, namely, the past; the corner of the mind where old impressions have been buried; something in the past which the dreamer doesn't want to be reminded of or look at too closely.

CHAIN · restrictions; links. "The chain that binds"; "a chain is only as strong as its weakest link"; "missing link."

CHALICE · (See *cup;* also *goblet* in Archetypes chapter)

CHANGING INTO ANOTHER PERSON · (See Dream Characters chapter)

CHASE · fleeing, or being chased by, self's creations.

CHIN · associated with talking. "Lead with your chin"; "chinning" (chatter); "take it on the chin." (See *appearance*)

CHINA OR CRYSTAL · something valuable. *Breaking of*—shattered ideals; broken faith. "Crystal clear."

CHRIST · (See Dream Characters and Archetypes chapters)

CIRCLE · eternity, Spirit, no beginning and no end; symbol of God. *Circular movement*—getting nowhere; aimlessness; a feeling of tension. "Going around in circles."

CIVIL WAR · inner conflict of lower self against higher self.

CLAWS · power to wound or destroy; defenses.

CLAY · something is ready to be molded or shaped. "Modeling clay"; "feet of clay" (weakness of character).

CLIFF · obstacles in life. Teetering on a cliff may mean danger to physical body or health, or warn of a spiritual fall. Look for play of words on proper name *Cliff*(ord).

CLIMBING · moving toward a goal; escape from a current problem; generally bettering oneself, socially or materially; spiritual achievement. To look down on others from a height may indicate the dreamer feels superior, "looks down on them."

CLOCK · with *hands still*—death; with *hands racing*—time running out; *alarm clock ringing*—warning. The dreamer may be objecting to "living by the clock." "Around the clock"; "clock out"; "clock watcher."

CLOTHES · as a rule represent levels of consciousness of the personality. The type of garment may refer to a particular activity, e.g., a *housedress* or other *work clothes* relate to one's work, *swim clothes* to relaxation, *formal attire* to formal thoughts, etc. Quality materials and clean, clear, beautiful colors are usually positive symbols. Inappropriate dress means something is wrong or that the dreamer is creating the wrong impression by failing to adhere to acceptable conduct; it could also be a literal criticism of the dreamer's own taste. *Clothing*—limitations of thought which envelop the ego (opinions, ideas, theories, habits, prejudices, etc.). *Spotted and soiled clothing*—impure attitudes. *Disheveled clothing*—disorderliness. (All of these may be literal messages.) *Clothing too tight*—dreamer may be "too tight" or "too mean" in thought and actions. *Toplessness* may indicate feminine freedom. (See other apparel under individual listings.)

CLOUDS · when delicate and feathery, a person without ideals or purposes, one who is easily swayed; impending difficulties. Note the color of the clouds. "Clouded vision"; "head in the clouds"; "on cloud nine"; "under a cloud." (See *smoke*)

COAT · warmth, love, protection. *Overcoat*—if it is raining, we need the protection of an overcoat or umbrella. (A dream in which the proper protective attire, such as a *raincoat*, is missing could be a warning about exposure to trouble, spiritual or physical.)

COBWEB · snare or trap; subtle entanglements; neglect; flimsy. "Cobwebs of the mind." (See *spider*, under "Insects," in Animals chapter)

COFFIN · possible death symbol; need or desire to bury a dead issue. Look for play on the word coughing. "Coffin nail" (cigarette).

COLD · may refer to respiratory infection; lacking in passion. "Left out in the cold"; "knocked cold." (See *ice*)

COMMUNION · mystical agreement; participation in the spiritual union; sharing. "Commune with God."

COMPASS · inner direction (instinct, intuition); finding right direction or guidance (material or spiritual).

CONCRETE · permanent; unyielding; obstinate; not abstract.

CONSTIPATION · need for cleansing; need to change eating habits; inner tension; withholding of feelings; lack of self expression or self esteem.

COOKING · an attempt to make life situations palatable; can relate to preparation of spiritual food. "Now you're cooking"; "cooking on the front burner" (doing it right); "cook your goose."

CORD/CHORD · look for the play on words; the "silver cord" (the connection between the finite and the infinite); the umbilical cord; music, harmony. "That struck a chord" (feelings or emotions).

CORNER · change of direction; meeting place; turning point in attitudes or approach. "Four corners of the earth"; "cut corners"; "rough corners"; "cornered."

CORPSE · outer self without the awareness of the divine spark within; something needs to be brought to life; death fears or wishes. (See *death*)

COSTUME · clothing we wear when we want to play-act; the character the dream may be calling attention to will be revealed by the type of costume. Can be a past-life recall. (See Dream Characters chapter)

COUNTRY · relaxation, openness. If a foreign country, someone or something foreign to dreamer. (See *field*)

CRATER · memory of old hurt; old emotions; frightening situation; awakening to new activity.

CRAWL · beginning of new activity; immaturity; may indicate desire to return to carefree days of childhood. If an adult is crawling, may refer to feelings of degradation, or a "degrading experience." "Crawl before you walk"; "I'll make you crawl."

CROSS · (See Archetypes chapter)

CROWD · anonymity; public opinion; camouflage. "Lost in the crowd." (See Dream Characters chapter)

CROWN · Christ symbol; wealth, power and authority. The highest chakra center according to Eastern philosophy, or the highest spiritual center according to the Edgar Cayce readings. (See "Spiritual Centers")

CRYING · if the dreamer awakes crying, take a good look at the dream and surrounding symbols; warning of trouble; inability to cry out or run away may indicate improper diet (the body is crying out for attention). Tears also play an important part in making one whole; sorrow over actions. "A crying need"; "for crying out loud"; "battle cry"; "crying over spilled milk"; "cry your eyes out"; "have a good cry."

CUP · receptivity. "My cup runneth over." (See *goblet* in Archetypes chapter)

CURB · where you park; it may be saying "move on," or "curb it."

CURLERS · something in your life that would "curl your hair."

CURVE-IN-THE-ROAD · rounding a bend in the road of life; a turning point.

CUTTING · separation of one thing or one person from another; fear of being cut down to size; desire to cut someone else down to size. "Cut that out"; "cut back"; "cut both ways"; "short cut"; "cutting remark"; "cutup"; "cut and dried"; "cut off"; "cut loose."

· D ·

DAM · something needs to be brought under control, perhaps emotions. (See *water* in Archetypes chapter)

DANCING · spontaneous expression of inner feeling of happiness; can be in step or out of step, harmonious or inharmonious movements; changes; sexual connotations; joyous. "I could have danced all night"; "dancing around"; "dance to another tune" (a change of attitude, opinion, or behavior).

DAWN · the beginning of a new cycle of life; the Higher Self (sun) is rising.

DAY · good; facing toward the source of light (See *A Search for God,* Book II*). *Sunny day*—all turns out well. *Cloudy day*—wrong doing, uncertainty, sorrow. "Choose this day whom ye will serve"; "see the light of day"; "the difference between day and night" (a big difference in things); "day after day"; "call it a day"; "day in day out."

DEAF · a desire not to know what is happening within; fear of hearing things we feel would hurt, or learning things we do not wish to face. "Turn a deaf ear."

DEATH · dreams of death can be literal if the person is not afraid of dying; may mean something in the dreamer's life is dying out. A change in consciousness, good or evil; a warning against doing

---

*Available from the A.R.E. Press, Virginia Beach, VA.

too much physically; desire to escape a difficult situation; hostile feelings for another. To dream of a person who is actually dead as if he or she were alive and normal may be an actual contact with that person. It may suggest that the person is still thought of and missed but no longer mourned. If the dead person beckons to the dreamer, it suggests the dreamer is depressed or the deceased may want to be joined. *Death symbols*—stopped clock (time has run out, especially if the hands are at midnight); a pair of scissors (divide while uniting, unite while dividing); a letter, a card or handkerchief edged in black; hour glass; fallen mirror; crossing a wide river; pulled tooth; attendance at a funeral; coffin; grave; ribbon or spray of flowers on the front door; curtains, as at the end of a play (white curtains to a person unafraid of dying); a large rolling river, or a muddy river. (See *deceased* in Dream Characters chapter)

DEBIT · past actions and thoughts that have not harmonized with your Spirit.

DEBT · similar to *debit*, but can also express the idea of not living up to the mark; a sin or trespass; not giving to others what they, in their life, have given to you. "Forgive us our debts as we forgive our debtors."

DEFECATE · (See *evacuation*)

DEFORMITY · part of your nature that, due to fear, repression, or ignorance, has not been able to grow in its natural beauty. (See Dream Characters chapter)

DELUGE · an overpowering release of emotion, as experienced in a nervous breakdown or shock. The Deluge at the time of Noah cleansed the earth of corruption.

DEMONS/DEVIL · (See Dream Characters chapter)

DEN (room) · (See Buildings chapter)

DESERT · barren of spiritual life; a call to improve relationships since deserts are associated with non-productiveness; an ancient symbol for the solitude of meditation; feelings of isolation; emotions or creativity have "gone dry."

DICE · fate, chance, luck, a gamble. "The die is cast"; "it's in the dice."

DIGGING · a desire to discover facts in a situation or relationship; a fear that something may be "dug up." "Dig in"; "to dig" (to understand).

DIORAMA · appreciation of an awakening of earthly beauty in three dimensions.

DIRT · something is "dirty"; guilt. May be a call to "clean up your act." Accumulation of prejudices and errors.

DISASTER · tornados, hurricanes, floods, wrecks, etc., may indicate how you feel about an area of your life. A natural disaster can mean adultery.

DISTRESS · a loved one who has passed on and is in distress is a call to prayer; dreamer may be experiencing a distressing period of life; *despair*—warning of wrong doing; *despondency*—warning of coming illness or trouble.

DIVORCE · cutting off your other half; separation of love (feminine) from wisdom (male), emotions from reason, intuition from intellect.

DOCUMENT · usually some important idea, or important information about oneself recorded for proof.

DOLL · a desire to return to carefree days of childhood; substitute figure for a child or a baby; an aspect of self that needs to be brought to life. A "doll" (a lovable person); "to doll up"; "living doll."

DREAMING · to dream that you are dreaming is called "lucid dreaming" (to be aware of yourself dreaming); can symbolize a contact with the innermost content of your being. (See Types of Dreams)

DRINK · offering from the Gods to those who are spiritually thirsty; mystical communion symbol. Take a look at the drink being offered; each drink has a meaning of its own. "Drink in"; "drink deep"; "drink to"; "come drink of the water of life."

DROWNING · literal, or it could refer to a physical condition, such as pneumonia or emphysema, depending on the context (lungs filling up); emotional tensions; dreamer may feel that life is overwhelming, that he or she is going under.

DRUMS · primitive urges relate to war drums of primitive man; also relate to the first spiritual center, in that drumming works on the gonads, the base of the life force. "Drummer" (salesperson); "drummed out of town"; "drum up business." (See Spiritual Centers chart)

DUSK · the end of a cycle of life; the Higher Self (sun) being obscured.

· E ·

EAR · related to hearing; reliance upon external guidance; signifies receptivity to inner guidance. "Now hear this"; "be all ears"; "lend an ear"; "to pin someone's ears back"; "turn a deaf ear"; "wet behind the ears"; "play by ear." (See *appearance)*

EARTH · element associated with the first spiritual center, gonads; material manifestation; plane from which people reason in the finite; lower self symbol; need to be tilling and sowing to produce. "Down to earth"; "earthy"; "four corners of the earth."

EARTHQUAKE · shake-up coming; a feeling of great change and a fear of "coming apart"; crumbling foundation; unstable conditions. "Earth-shaking."

EATING · your diet may need to be changed; need or desire for spiritual nourishment. To dream of constantly eating may signify dissatisfaction with spiritual progress; a wish to satisfy a basic need. "Eat your words"; "eat your heart out."

EGGS · new birth; something hatching; some believe it to be a symbol of diety. To break the shell may be saying "you are coming out of your shell." "To suck an egg" (trying to teach one with experience or an older person); "he laid an egg" (failing in one's performance); "walk on eggs" (proceed with caution); "good egg"; "egg head"; "don't put all your eggs in one basket."

EGYPT · biblically it means "bondage"; ancient Egypt also represents time in history when physical perfection was of great concern. Since the root of *gypsy* is Egypt, you could question whether you have a purpose in life or are just roaming around.

ELEVATOR · *ascending* may be bringing contents from the unconscious up into the conscious mind; also a suggestion that a rising in some area of the dreamer's life is taking place; *descending* carries a connotation of failure, but it may designate delving into the subconscious; *standing still* may mean the dreamer feels immobilized or is not going anywhere and is in need of a change; *up and down,* indecision. "Straight and narrow."

ERASER · eliminate faults, erase mistakes. "Minimize the faults, accentuate the virtues."

ESCAPE · a desire for improved conditions; a way out.

EVACUATION · letting go; being delivered of worries and responsibilities; being purged of guilt and repressions, being liberated from inhibition. "On a potty in velvet pants" (not really letting go, according to the Edgar Cayce readings).

EXAMINATION · physical or written test you may be facing in a particular situation, so be prepared; could relate to a test in your spiritual life.

EXCREMENT · worry over a supposedly unclean activity or thought; a cleansing or need for cleansing of inner feelings, such as guilt, inhibitions, resentments, hate, worry, or fear.

EXPLOSION · change in consciousness from an explosive to a peaceful state; warning of hostile feelings which may be destructive.

EXPOSURE · state of undress in public is a warning dream, even if the nudity is unseen by others, which merely suggests that others are not aware of the error or shortcoming. (See *naked*)

EYES · awareness; mental perception. *Bandaged*—unprejudiced, inexperienced; *wink of the eye*—either approval or deception; *red eyes*—drunkenness; *loss of eyesight*—loss of insight and enlightenment; *to find eyeglasses*—could indicate the development of insights, depending on context; *single eye* (all-seeing eye, as on the American dollar bill)—singleness of purpose. Look for play on word "I." Windows of the soul; the "I am" (God within). "If thine eye be single, thy whole body will be filled with light"; "eye for an eye"; "keep your eyes open for"; "easy on the eyes."

· F ·

FACE · what you present to others; *hiding face*, shame. "Face down"; "face up"; "wear a long face"; "lose face"; "save face"; "bold face."

FAIRY TALES · usually tell of a transmutation taking place. A method for preserving "truths" in the earth. (See "Snow White and the Seven Dwarfs")

FALLING · fear of failure in some area; not living up to accepted moral standards; lack of support or solid base; falling into sin. "Fall back"; "fall flat on your face"; "to fall for"; "fall short"; "fall in love."

FAT · sometimes relates to pregnancy; sometimes lack of will, as in overeating. "A fat chance"; "chew the fat"; "the fat of the land."

FEATHER · chivalry; cowardice; transitory character of life; *flying* *feathers*, confusion. "A feather in your hat"; "to show the white feather" (cowardice); "to feather your nest."

FEED/FEEDING · to dispense truth and goodness; teaching; can relate to the feeding of spiritual food.

FEET · understanding; *barefooted*, true understanding; *defective feet*, defective pathway. "Feet of clay"; "feet on the ground"; "sweep you off your feet."

FEMALE · feeling, emotional side of our nature. (See Dream Characters chapter)

FENCE · (See Buildings chapter)

FEVER · (See *fire* in Archetypes chapter)

FIELD · expansion; opportunity; room for growth; green, fresh, vigor of life; abundance; prosperity. "Out in the open"; "play the field"; "out in left field."

FIGHTING · warring with self or others.

FINDING MONEY OR VALUABLES · an incentive or reward for efforts toward spiritual fulfillment. May be suggesting how to make money, depending on surrounding symbols.

FINGERS · *thumb*—"all thumbs"; "green thumb"; "thumbs up or down"; *wagging of the index finger* is a warning or a reproach; *pointing finger* could mean self being accused. "Snap your fingers"; "slip through your fingers"; "fingers in the pie"; "put the finger on."

FIRE · (See Archetypes chapter)

FIREPLACE · comfort; purification; digestion; a place to burn up the dross.

FIREWORKS · celebration; emotional upheavals on display. "Going off like a Roman candle"; "hot as a firecracker."

FLAG · signaling device used to attract attention; patriotism; standards; *white flag*, surrender; debts.

FLAME · old love, passion, sweetheart, zeal; to burst into flame can be anger or love, depending on other symbols or size of flame; a large flame, to be engulfed. "My old flame." (See *fire* in Archetypes chapter)

FLEE · being chased by one's creations; avoiding problems.

FLOODS · uncontrolled emotions; cleansing the body of earthy desires, as in "The Great Flood," or Deluge. "Flooded with problems" (flooded emotions). (See *deluge*)

FLOWERS · expressive of the fruits of the spirit. If they are unappreciated or neglected, there is an indication of neglected or latent abilities. *Dying flowers* could denote a spiritual deficiency; *healthy flowers* tell us we are enjoying vitality, beauty, and the blossoming or full bloom of the individual, often through some new relationship involving love and tenderness; *crushed flowers*, defloration, loss of virginity; *dried flowers*, preserving one's love instead of giving it out. *Blue flowers*—flowers of the soul, the mystical, the romantic or lyrical (for additional significance of colors in flowers, see Color chapter). *Clover*—better known for their leaves, three leaves in one, the Trinity; *four leaf clover*—luck; *lily*—innocence, and incorruptible nature (lily white); *rose*—perfection, Christ spirit; *tulip*—harbinger of spring, a new beginning; *daisy*—fresh, first-rate quality. *Blossoms*—new life, beauty, expectation, unfoldment; *flower of youth*—virginity.

FLYING · wishful thinking; astral projection; suggests rising above the problem. A wish to escape the pull of the earth and limitations imposed by nature (keeping an eye on reality); flights of fancy and the mind. Transformation, like the caterpillar changing into a butterfly and flying. To be suspended in the air may indicate being "up in the air" about a nagging problem, or it may be saying "get both feet on the ground."

FOG · a hazy, obscured view; mental confusion. "Don't have the foggiest notion" (don't known which way to turn). *Foghorn*— warning of impending danger; *fog-light*—seeing better in a confusing situation; trying to improve perception.

FOOD · related to diet; spiritual nourishment. *Meat* is flesh, the sensual and sexual side of living, the sins of the flesh, the carcass without the living spirit. (See *meat*.) To serve food to others may symbolize serving others spiritual nourishment. *Beef*—the strong, "beefy"; *chicken*—cowardly; *hams*—thighs; *sweets*—sweetheart; *fruit*—work which is "bearing fruit" (a fruitful period of development). After the flower, the blossoming of the individual, comes the *fruit* (a later and more mature phase of the individual's life). *Stealing apples*—trying to procure a love that doesn't rightfully belong to the dreamer; a desire for someone who is already claimed by another.

FOREHEAD · location of the third eye, symbol of clairvoyance and vision; psychic energy; up-front thinking; high intelligence.

FOREST · inner darkness, feeling lost, confusion; world of the unconscious; need for inner transformation, need to find oneself. (See *woods*)

FORK · to pick out carefully. Division, as *fork in the road or river*, means a time to choose. "Fork over"; "fork out"; "forked tongue" (lies or insincerity).

FORMAL ATTIRE · can mean "stepping out"; being in a proper situation.

FORTS · symbolize a defensive attitude toward life; warring, defensive emotional state.

FOUNTAIN · water of life, Truth. "Fountain of youth" (longevity).

FROST · matter which in itself is lifeless, solid and inert, a state of latency. May mean spiritual life needs to thaw out. (See *ice, snow*)

FRUIT · trees laden with fruit often represent a fruitful life. The destruction of fruit has negative connotations; fruit with lots of seeds, as a watermelon, can be related to "planting the seed, while God grants the increase" (if surrounding colors or associated colors are black, your efforts are wasted). Results of labor, reward, accomplishment, discipline, effort, training, transmutation, "fruits of labor." Absence of fruit where it would be natural to find it, as at a fruit stand, means "fruitless"—disappointment, unfavorable result, emptiness, not worth the effort. "Peachy" (a wonderful, colorful personality); "by their fruits they shall be known" (Matthew 7:16–20). (See *food*)

FUNERAL · a death symbol; can mean death of an old part of self, an awakening to the new. (See *death*)

· G ·

GAMBLING · taking a chance with life, friendships, or business.

GARBAGE · *pail/disposal*—something needs to be eliminated; cleansing necessary; may be a need to take a look at the "garbage" in one's life. *Garbage truck*—vehicle that takes the garbage away.

GARDEN · where things grow, good or bad; the inner life of an individual; cultivating personality traits. The garden may be orderly or disorderly, representing different aspects of the mind. A desire or need to cultivate something, a new talent, a new interest, a family, a new friendship, etc. If the garden is overgrown with brambles or choked with weeds, certain parts of the person are not likely to grow or thrive. A privileged and secluded place where man and woman hope to find harmony and love. *Garden of Eden*—the pure state of consciousness, the first state, the lost paradise from which we have parted.

GATES · may lead to the unconscious, or to the object of the dreamer's desire. *Opening a gate*—a way through to the conscious mind; *garden gates*—gates to paradise where one may hope to find one's heart's desire. "Pearly gates" (gates to heaven).

GIFT · something being given to you. Gifts of the wise men to Christ: *gold*—purity of body (perfection); *frankincense*—wisdom or devotion of the mind; *myrrh*—surrender of mind to spirit. "Don't look a gift horse in the mouth"; "the gift without the giver is bare."

GLACIER · large accumulation of frozen areas of consciousness, or feelings seemingly impossible to dissolve. (See *ice*)

GLANDS · *swollen glands*—disease or infection in some aspect of the dreamer's life. (See Spritual Centers chart)

GLASSES · (See *eyes*)

GLITTER · an encouragement that things will be "brighter"; brightness, shining, glistening. "All that glitters is not gold."

GLOVE · protection for hands, which represent the kind of work you do. "Handle with kid gloves"; "throw down the glove."

GOBLET · (See Archetypes chapter)

GORGE · a good example of how dream symbols work: dreams of a narrow mountain pass between two mountains (a gorge) are related in a physiological way to the human body—the narrow passage in the throat area. Hence, gorges may represent a departure from or neglect of the moral way by such abuses of the body as alcoholism, overeating, sensuality, or any other thing that is ultimately harmful and that represents a kind of selfish "gorging."

GRAIL · (See *goblet* in Archetypes chapter)

GRAVE · to impress deeply; heavy, serious situation; a reminder to bury what is dead. "Grave illness"; "a grave matter"; "calling from the grave."

GUM · sticky situation; tacky; *chewing gum*, something to "chew on."

GUNS · emotional explosions; taking aim. A man approaching with a knife or gun can be a sex symbol; something or someone is being "shot down." "Jump the gun"; "stick to your guns."

GYPSIES · (See Dream Characters chapter, also *Egypt*)

· H ·

HAIL · hardening of emotions or ideas. "Hail fellow, well met" (sociable or friendly); "hail to the king."

HAIR · because hair comes from the head, it stands for thoughts; the different types of hair represent different kinds of thoughts. *Kinky hair*—kinky thinking; *curly hair*—something to "make your hair curl"; *blonde hair*—golden thoughts; *black hair*—negative thoughts or mysterious thoughts; *white hair*—wisdom; *bright red hair*—temper; *golden red hair*—constructive, active mind; *bald head*—lack of thoughts; *haircut*—a new way of thinking. If a young, long haired person is asked to cut her hair, it could mean she is being asked to cut her ideals. Hairstyles can also indicate kinds of mental activity, for example, *forward sweep*—too forward; *disheveled hair*—mental confusion; *wig*—false thinking; *new hair style*—new approach.

HALO · a mandala indicating saintliness. (See *mandala* in Archetypes chapter)

HAMMER · instrument for building; a driving force.

HANDKERCHIEF · may be a forewarning of an oncoming cold; edged in black, it is a possible death symbol.

HANDS · represent kinds of service; *beautiful hands*—beautiful and creative work; *right hand*—control (it is the positive, masculine, executive side); *left hand*—negative, feminine, receptive; *pointed downward*—the physical nature; *pointed upward*—a spiritual situation. *Shaking hands*—friendship, or meet yourself; *applauding hands*—encouragement and approval, unless negative symbols appear with them, which might indicate egotism; *hands folded in prayer*—a call to prayer, or you need to be thankful for something; *unclean hands* may show guilty conscience for "dirty work" being done; *rough hands* could show a lack of gentleness toward others. Hands which resemble claws may refer to the animal characteristics of scratching, clawing, grasping, and holding on, or wounding. "Hands down"; "hands off"; "hard hand"; "show your hand"; "lend a helping hand"; "openhanded" (generous); "cut your hand off" (don't steal). (See *left*)

HARP · persistently "harping on" something; associated with the music of the angels; spiritual achievement.

HARVEST · a particular plan or project may be ready to "harvest."

HATE · self-hatred.

HATS · often represent the thinking process and the state of mind or the personality; *fur hat*—fuzzy thinking; *black hats*—bad guys because black symbolizes the mysteries associated with the unknown forces manifested in man through the superconscious; *white hats*—good guys because white is the color of purity. (See also Color chapter.) "Wearing many hats" means having several professions, and each tells its own story—*fireman's hat, policeman's, nurse's, hard hats,* etc. "Pass the hat"; "talk through your hat"; "keep it under your hat"; "take your hat off to"; "toss your hat in the ring."

HEAD · the center of the intellect, and so it represents thoughts; a head rolling down the road or a headless person appearing in a dream may be saying "don't loose your head" over a situation. *Head on backwards*—preconceived ideas or prejudices which hamper progress; *bald head* could mean no ideals or thoughts; an *oddly shaped head*—"egg head"; "square head"; "big head"; "shrunken head." "Off the top of my head"; "hold your head up high"; "come to a head"; "head over heels"; "over your head"; "get it through your head"; "turn one's head"; "heads up."

HEADLIGHTS · (See Vehicles chapter)

HEART · the *"heart center"* (see Spiritual Centers chart)—the fourth spiritual center, the center of love and intuition; *valentine*—sweetheart. "Don't let your heart run away with your head"; "wearing your heart on your sleeve"; "the heart of the matter"; "have a heart"; "heavy heart"; "after your heart"; "change of heart"; "from the bottom of my heart"; "break your heart"; "my heart's in my mouth"; "open-hearted" (sincere).

HIDING · What is the dreamer hiding? Can be related to the wish to return to the womb; maybe something needs to be brought out in the open or needs to be hidden.

HILL · *going up a steep hill*—progress (on the way up); *downhill*—not in control, difficulty to be overcome. "Over the hill"; "the going is all uphill."

HOLES · bag or pocket with holes could mean money unwisely spent. "Full of holes" (uncertainties); "a hole in the wall"; "burn a hole in your pocket"; "in the hole."

HOLY LAND · hopes and ideals; holy state. (See Archetypes chapter)

HOME · dreams of conditions back home, or where you used to live, are usually emblems of conditions left behind. "Back home"; "home to the father"; "home free"; "home is where the heart is"; "something to write home about." (See *house* in Buildings chapter)

HONEY · (See *bread*) predigested food, or application of spiritual food or laws. "Honey of an idea."

HORN · horns are used to warn of danger, but can also be used to express triumph. Since *animal horns* protrude from the head and are used for defense, they can suggest a negative attitude. "Don't blow your own horn"; "horn of plenty"; "horny"; "Gabriel, come blow your horn"; "lock horns"; "pull in your horns."

HOUR GLASS · possible death symbol, as in time running out; related to an "hour glass" figure.

HURRICANE · hurried, overwrought mind; mental pressure. (See *air*)

· I ·

ICE · chilled, frozen feelings or attitudes; incapable of feeling and loving; insensitive to truth and law; cold areas of consciousness. It may just be saying "thaw out"; it can also be related to fear. "Icy fingers up and down my spine"; "makes the chills come"; slang for diamonds; "put it on ice"; "break the ice"; "on thin ice."

ILLNESS · an emotional or psychological ailment. "You make me sick"; "ill at ease" (dis-ease).

IMPRISON · behavior patterns can imprison both mentally and physically. This pattern might be an unbalanced diet which, if carried to extremes, could imprison the body through illness. May also refer to continually negative attitudes that eventually imprison the mind and spirit. Something may need to be set free.

INFECTIONS · wounds, eruptions, boils, or infections can be warnings regarding physical health. Long red streaks indicate blood poisoning. Something festering within.

INJURY · self-punishment or guilt feelings; hurt feelings.

INK · writing or communications. "Inkling" (vague idea).

INTOXICATION · dreamer may have a drinking problem; a stupefying of the lower nature by a sudden influx of the higher nature (spirit) for which the lower is unprepared.

ISLAND · loneliness; isolation; someone too concerned with the subconscious and who needs to be more conscious of reality (sea of the unconscious); a limited state. "No man is an island unto himself."

IVORY · purity, strength, and power because ivory comes from the elephant. "Ivories" (slang for teeth, or piano keys); "living in an ivory tower" (impractical; detached).

· J ·

JELLO · could mean that you should eat more gelatin; uncertain, no spine.

JERUSALEM · heart of truth.

JOURNEYS · (See Vehicles chapter)

JUNGLE · usually denotes confusion or an uncivilized state of being.

· K ·

KEYS · power, authority; solution to a problem. *A key in a lock*— possible sex symbol, or can mean unlocking something in the dreamer; basic importance, as in the "key issue." "Keys to the kingdom"; "key to the city"; "key up"; "key position."

KILL · can mean killing that part of self associated with person being killed. "Killing with kindness"; "in at the kill."

KNEES · weakness; may be calling your attention to the fact that you need to pray. "Weak in the knees"; "knee deep"; "knee high"; "bring someone to their knees."

KNIFE · can be a sex symbol. A man approaching with a knife could be a warning against "free love" (cut out sex). "Cut it out"; "under the knife"; "knife in the back."

KNOCK · may be the Christ spirit knocking and waiting to be received at the door of the heart; criticism. "Knock about"; "knock it off"; "don't knock it 'til you've tried it"; "knock cold"; "knock down"; "opportunity knocking."

· L ·

LADDER · down or up, related to goals. "Jacob's Ladder" (God reveals himself to Jacob); "ladder of success."

LAMP · a source of spiritual strength, wisdom, and enlightenment; understanding. "Put a little light on the subject." (See *light* in Archetypes chapter)

LATE · near the end; a synonym for the deceased. "It's later than you think."

LAUGHTER · concentrate more on the bright side of life, be more carefree. "Laughing up his sleeve"; "laughing on the outside, crying on the inside"; "laugh it off"; "no laughing matter"; "laughing out of the other side of your mouth"; "had the last laugh."

LEFT · the passive or feeling, feminine side of life; what you left behind, perhaps karma or the past; wrong way. Whether a person is left or right handed, he or she is not going "the right way" when the left way comes up in a dream. Incoming energy. "Leftist" (liberal).

LEGS · the support system to spiritual foundations; *legless*—poor foundation in efforts to deal with a current problem or activity; seeing another person legless shows poor insight into what the other person represents. "Get up on your hind legs"; "shake a leg"; "give a leg up"; "no leg to stand on"; "you're pulling my leg"; "on your last leg."

LETTER · a message coming; if lined in black, a possible death symbol; a letter that is soiled or has dirt on it may refer to a letter in which someone is doing a dirty trick, such as a "Dear John" letter.

LIGHT · (See Archetypes chapter)

LIGHTNING · may be suggesting a need to be well grounded; sudden illumination. *Lightning of the Lord*—possible warning of trouble. "Quick as lightning"; "lightning never strikes twice."

LIGHTHOUSE · guide to safety; warning of a dangerous area; sign of life and activity.

LIMB · in a man's dream, loss of a limb can suggest castration, or the feeling that someone is castrating you. In a woman the meaning could be loss of virginity. *Being dismembered*—the individual's life may be breaking up. Any branch, outgrowth, or extension of a larger body.

LINE · *vertical*—active/positive; masculine; *horizontal*—passive/negative; feminine; *wavy*—indecision. "Side line"; "draw the line"; "lay it on the line"; "read between the lines"; "to line one's pockets."

LIPS · related to speech. "My lips are sealed"; "hot lips"; "keep a stiff upper lip"; "button your mouth." (See *mouth*)

LOSING VALUABLES · losing spiritual values or a warning of possible theft; sometimes in dreams it turns up as losing your wallet. *Lost key*—lost way.

LOTUS BLOSSOM · (See Archetypes chapter)

LUMPS · things may be "rough" (not running smoothly). "Take your lumps"; "lump in your throat"; "if you don't like it, you can lump it."

· M ·

MANA/MANNA · The prayer "give us this day our daily bread" is referring to the spiritual food supplied miraculously for our spiritual nourishment, such as was given to the Israelites on their journey through the wilderness; what Christ was referring to when he said "I have bread ye know not of."

MANDALA · (See Archetypes chapter)

MAP · detailed guide leading toward a desired destination; plans; patterns of experiences in code. "Put on the map"; "your map" (your face).

MARRIAGE · (See Archetypes chapter)

MEAT · higher qualities which sustain the soul. "The meat of the matter."

MERRY-GO-ROUND · fun; pleasure; an opportunity to get the brass ring. "Make the round go merry"; "on a merry-go-round"; "going around in circles."

METAL/MEDAL · strength and durability; recognition of achievement.

MILK · immaturity; calling attention to diet: the body might need milk as a supply of calcium. "Milk of human kindness"; "milk of life"; "don't cry over spilt milk"; "to milk dry."

MIRRORS · reflection of self; a fallen mirror could be a death symbol. "Face yourself"; "reflect on this"; "mirror image"; "looking glass."

MOAN · may be calling attention to distresses of the inner self, or activities of self; the body crying out for a change in diet.

MONEY · at the highest level, a symbol for spiritual graces; on a material level, nothing more than itself; at its worst, the price we are paying for self-indulgence; a lowering of moral standards; misadventures; what something will cost you. "Money is the root of all evil"; "in the money"; "money's worth"; "money bags."

MOON · symbol of the female principle; the reflection of the sun; celestial bodies represent spiritual ideals. "Moonlighting"; "shoot for the moon"; "mooning around"; "reach for the moon."

MORPHINE · destructive addiction.

MOUNTAIN · (See Archetypes chapter)

MOUTH · *Enlarged mouth*—associated with "you have a big mouth." "Big mouth"; "mouth off"; "foot in mouth." (See *appearance; also lips, teeth*, etc.)

MOVE · inability to move or cry out—wrong diet (associated with constipation). (See *paralysis*)

MOVIE · a projection of self's attitudes; re-run of past events. May be suggesting less observation and more action. "Get the picture."

MUD · departure from or neglect of the moral way; often related to physical abuses of the body, such as alcoholism, sensuality, or over-eating. Muddy water is sometimes a death symbol, or perhaps your spiritual life is muddied up; confused thinking. "Mudslinging."

MUSIC · harmony; singing or hearing sacred, beautiful music indicates harmonized activity of divine forces in self; *music of the spheres*—being in balance with the universe; divine influences in life; *musical instruments*—artistic achievements; high vibrations; balance as in the eighty-eight keys of the piano. (See *eight* in Numbers chapter.) "Face the music."

· N ·

NAIL · *filing finger nails*—trimming the rough edges of self; taking care of the details. "Hard as nails"; "hit the nail on the head"; "nail down."

NAKED · freedom from the constriction (garments) of "earthy" self; lacking thoughts; undisguised; guiltless; stripped of faith; warning of being exposed. "Naked truth"; "bare facts"; "barely there."

NAMES · *one's own name being called*—a "calling" to a specific endeavor, often spiritually oriented. (See *famous people* in Dream Characters chapter)

NATIVE · uncivilized manner; *native country*—where you are from.

NEWSPAPER · message or information concerning daily life.

NIGHT · the period of darkness; a state of ignorance, or being unenlightened; in dreams nightlife may refer to what is going on in your dreams; state of depression. *Night and day* may refer to the cycles of life.

NOSE · (See *appearance*)

NUT · may be related to going within to find the seed. "A nut to crack" (a problem to solve); "in a nutshell"; "nutty."

· O ·

OASIS · place of refuge; quenching of a "thirst"; growth in the midst of barrenness.

OCEAN · subconscious and superconscious areas of the mind; water representing the spirit of life, the ocean becomes the largest body of spiritual life. Mysteries of the deep; overpowering emotions. "Oceans of love." (See *water* in Archetypes chapter)

ODOR · if a bad odor, something "smells"; on the other hand, if the odor is sweet or fragrant it could have the opposite meaning. "Heavenly odor."

OFFICE · a work environment, look for the special association related to that activity. "Get to work", "office wife"; "I gave at the office."

OIL · remove the friction by "oiling"; a situation or relationship found beneath the surface. *Oil well*—extract the "riches." "Oily" (flattering speech; pious); "oil the palm" (to bribe).

ONION · *peeling an onion*—take a closer look at something you are crying over; *onion pack*—an old-fashioned remedy for asthma, bronchitis, common cold, congestion, pneumonia. If one of these conditions is present, dream may be suggesting that you use an onion pack. "Something to cry about."

ORANGE · if a fruit, it may be saying "eat more oranges" or showing a need for Vitamin C. (See Color chapter)

ORCHARD · cultivated thoughts or ideas. "Fruits of your labor."

OUTSIDE · out in the open. "On the outside looking in."

· P ·

PAIN · physical or mental trouble or distress.

PALM · a palm leaf could be a pun, meaning you have "in the palm of your hand" something you have been wanting, perhaps not realizing it. *Palm tree*—unfolding of spiritual forces; *Palm Sunday*—symbolic of a victory, a winning, a triumph or joy.

PARACHUTE · depending on context, it could mean slow down. "Bail out" (you have protection).

PARALYSIS · being unable to move, rooted to the spot, frozen, immobile—conflicting impulses or emotions. The mind must awaken to the right concepts lest the higher self be paralyzed or distorted. The dreamer is longing to do something but is immobilized by fear of the consequences; or the dreamer longs to run from whatever is pursuing, but unconsciously desires it; the dreamer can't move because he or she doesn't want to. This conflict of wanting to face something but at the same time longing to flee from it often arises where there is a strong sexual attraction mingled with disgust. The physical inability to move signifies a mental block or inhibition, some aspect of the character is unwilling to move. Possibly the person is torn between ambition and laziness. May also refer to constipation (look at the background of the dream). A feeling of impotence, not being able to consciously control certain behavior. Unable to move legs—making no progress.

PAST · receding objects may denote the past; sometimes the past is depicted as an ancient dwelling, ancient clothing, old things, or an old person, a date in history or a scene from childhood; things left behind.

PATH · path of life; surrounding symbols will indicate whether yours may be beautiful, difficult, etc.

PEANUTS · small growth, protein.

PEN · writing or communications; the different types of pens have different meanings—*a fountain pen* can be a sex symbol; *a ball point pen* (designed after the joints of the body) could call attention to one of your joints. "The pen is mightier than the sword"; "penned in."

PENCIL · writing or communications; *pencil point*—"get the point" of the meaning; *pointed objects inserted into openings* may be sex symbols. "Point the way"; "boiling point"; "beside the point"; "make a point of"; "to stretch the point."

PENNY · a medium of exchange. "A copper"; "penny for your thoughts"; "your two cents' worth"; "penny wise and pound foolish"; "a bad penny" (someone or something undesirable); "a pretty penny" (a considerable sum of money); "turn an honest penny" (to earn one's living honestly); "penny-a-line."

PHONOGRAPH RECORD · may represent degrees of harmony and wholeness. "Broken record" (playing over and over).

PIANO · harmony and balance (eighty-eight keys). (See *eight* in Numbers chapter)

PICNIC · suggests a relaxed or physically pleasing atmosphere. "It's no picnic."

PICTURES · *of self*—self examination required; *taking a picture*—bring into focus or take a closer look at something. If *black and white*—see both sides; if in *color*—something colorful in your life.

PIT · warning of a fall or trap. "Pitfall"; "it's the pits."

PLANETS · spiritual ideals because of the heights they represent. (See Spiritual Centers chart for influences of planets on the body through the seven spiritual centers)

PLANT · If the plant is healthy and green, you are enjoying a healthy growth in life, perhaps a spiritual growth; dying or dried up—look for a spiritual deficiency.

PLASTIC · false; malleable. "Plastic society" (spending money we don't have by using charge cards).

POINT · (See *pencil*; also Sex chapter)

POISON · *skull & crossbones*—a warning of illness or death if something is taken internally; something may be tainting or destroying physical or mental health.

POOL · pool of life; relating to spirit only in a small way, hence the message may be to put forth greater effort in spiritual pursuits. (See *water* in Archetypes chapter)

PORT · safety; relaxation; new experiences; the dreamer may be "harboring" feelings or emotions that need to be out in the open. *Porthole*—take a closer look; *portside*—left side. "Any port in a storm."

PREGNANCY · to nourish and bring forth something new and precious.

PURSE · symbol of personal identity; *losing a purse*—losing valuables or identification; *clutching purse*—hanging on to valuables.

PYRAMID · a symbol of antiquity and mystery; a method of making a profit; secrets, mysteries of the initiates.

· Q ·

QUEEN · (See "Snow White and the Seven Dwarfs"; also, Dream Characters chapter)

QUAKE · something in your life is "earth-shaking"; vibrations raised to a trembling stage.

QUICKSAND · sinking; yielding to pressure.

· R ·

RADIO · pertains to sense of hearing; transmitting or receiving messages; communication. "Tune in"; "tune out"; "he who has an ear, let him hear."

RAIN · cleansing process within the spiritual life; sorrow or depression; spiritual nourishment. "Rain check"; "into each life a little rain must fall"; "put something away for a rainy day."

RAINBOW · God's promise to people that the earth would not be destroyed by flood again; the entire spectrum, meaning white light (high vibrations). (See *ark;* also Archetypes chapter)

RAPE · forceable, unwanted union with a negative aspect; warning of an undesirable union, such as joining a cult. (See Sex chapter)

RAQUET · look for the literal meaning and then for a possible play on words: is the dreamer involved in a questionable activity? or making "noise" about something?

RAZOR · a means of making self presentable; an instrument for cutting. "Razor sharp."

REFRIGERATOR · part of the spiritual life is still in cold storage; *freezer*, same thing, only processed for a longer period of time.

REFUSE · neglect of higher principles; *at one's door*—"sin lieth at thy door"; something may need to be discarded.

RESURRECTION · spiritual awakening; reincarnation; something "dead" needs to be brought back to life.

REVELATION · revealing the creative forces flowing through the body.

RIBBON · possible death symbol if on the front door; *cutting a ribbon*—a celebration or initiation; *yellow ribbon* may signify "welcome home"; *"blue ribbon"* (a winner).

RIGHT · the right side sometimes indicates action or "the right way"; the right side of a scene could relate to the future; active, masculine, or out-going energy. "To put things right"; "right-wing" (conservative); "in your right mind."

RING · the circle is a symbol for God; it represents eternity, no beginning and no end; unity and harmony; *wedding ring*—dreamer has taken a "vow" to self; also symbolic of the feminine accepting the masculine—the finger being inserted in the ring. "Ring of laughter"; "ring a bell"; "run rings around."

RIVER · (See Archetypes chapter)

ROAD · the individual way or destiny, leading to the realization of one's aims and objectives; *walking on a road*—the road of life (taking it step by step); *traveling in a vehicle*—reaching one's destination more quickly; *narrow road*—the path to heaven is straight and narrow; *going backward*—going backward in life, not making progress; *a fork in the road*—a choice between the right and wrong way, or a parting from someone or from old ways; *a roadblock*—an impediment in self; *a stretch of road*—period of time (the part already covered is the past and the road that lies ahead is the future); *a choice of roads*—alternative courses of action; *high or low road*—the idealistic way versus the selfish way; *crossroads*—a union of opposites, the meeting of two conflicting ways; *a turn in the road*—new events lie ahead; *a track to one side of the road*—being "side-tracked" from one's objective or "going off the beaten track" to try something unusual or original; *a cul-de-sac or dead end*—a road that leads nowhere; *a curve-in-the-road*—rounding a bend in the road of life. "One for the road"; "take to the road"; "the end of the road."

ROCK · often symbolizes the obstacles in life; unyielding; sturdy;

stable. "Rock of ages"; "solid as a rock"; "head hard as a rock"; "rock bottom"; "rocks" (slang for diamonds); "on the rocks." (See *stone* in Archetypes chapter)

ROLLER COASTER · speed; thrill; may be referring to drugs; someone or something else in control. "Going for a roller-coaster ride" (a quick temporary thrill).

ROPE · feeling "tied up"; a lack of freedom. "At the end of my rope"; "give him plenty of rope"; "roped in"; "know the ropes"; "on the ropes" (near collapse or ruin). ,

ROSE · beauty and love, perfection. (See Color chapter for specific meanings; also see *thorn*)

RUIN · could symbolize one's life in a state of decay or dilapidation.

RUNNING · getting into trouble; running from a problem; a need to exercise; hurried life style. *Running late*—it's later than you think. "Running around in circles"; "in the running"; "out of the running."

· S ·

SALT · zest for life; ancient symbol of wisdom; it preserves and flavors. "Salt of the earth"; "not worth your salt"; "salty" (coarse or earthy); "above or below the salt."

SAND · poor foundation; poor building material; irritating or abrasive; symbol for time. *Sand bag*—can be used as a weapon or fortification; *sand dollar*—has a five-pointed star on the outside and several doves inside, hence relates to the star of David and peace; *sandpaper*—used to smooth or polish. "Sands of time"; "time running out" (the hour glass).

SCALES · the seventh sign of the Zodiac (Libra); justice; balance; weighing good against evil; concern about overweight or underweight. "Turn the scales." (See *seven* in Numbers chapter)

SCALP · a foreign object in the scalp could indicate alien thinking that might provoke problems. To "scalp" (buy or sell for a quick profit).

SCISSORS · to separate; may be saying "cut it out"; can be a death symbol because it divides by uniting and unites by dividing. *Scissors-kick*—a method of swimming.

SCRATCH · *scratching self*—scarring or hurting spiritual self; to withdraw an entry in sports. "If it itches, scratch it"; "from scratch"; "scratch the surface"; "up to scratch."

SCYTHE · to cut or harvest earthly endeavors.

SEA · collective unconscious; a change in the surface of the sea could be a change in emotional climate; depths of the sea, depths of the mind. "At sea"; "follow the sea"; "go to sea"; "lost at sea." (See *ocean;* also *water* in Archetypes chapter)

SEASONS · *spring*—newness of life; *summer*—period of finest development; *autumn*—past maturity or middle life, colorful; *winter*—a time of latency and fruitlessness, cold. "Spring is in the air"; "sunny summer day"; "autumn of your life"; "a short winter's day."

SEED · germs of thoughts, ideals, desires; offspring; teaching; prosperity; new beginnings; the source or origin. "You plant the seed, God grants the increase"; "seed money."

SEW · something needs mending; something is mended; sewing something new, creating something new in one's life. Look for the play on word "sow" ("as ye sow so shall ye reap").

SHACK · poor dwelling place. "Shacking up" (living without moral code).

SHAMPOO · to dream of shampooing one's hair may be an indication that one either needs to clean up or is cleaning up his thinking.

SHIELD · a way of protection, prevention or defense; resistance.

SHOES · because worn on the feet, they can mean spiritual foundations (*under stand*ing), or basic principles; *nurses' white* shoes may symbolize a good foundation based on service to others; *overshoes, stockings, boots*—things worn on the feet, just as they bring protection to the physical body, often represent spiritual ideas and the protection they afford; *dirty shoes* may indicate unhealthy foundations; *sole* (soul) could relate to your spiritual life; *horseshoe*—good luck. "These boots were meant for walking"; "don't criticize your brother until you walk a mile in his moccasins"; "if the shoe fits, wear it"; "in another's shoes"; "fill one's shoes"; "the shoe is on the other foot."

SHOOTING · someone shooting you down, or you shooting someone else down; warning against being drawn into arguments that bring retorts or trouble. "Shoot the works"; "shot in the dark";

"give it your best shot"; "call the shots"; "a shot in the arm"; "like a shot"; "take a shot at."

SHORT · cut down to size; in reference to reincarnation, may mean you almost reached perfection in another life, but in some respect fell short; *shorts*—immature consciousness (they are usually associated with children). "Cut it short"; "come up short"; "shortcut"; "short end of the stick"; "in short." (See Dream Characters chapter)

SHOWING OFF · (See *naked*)

SITTING DOWN · sitting down on the job; relax. "Sitting hen."

SKATING · *roller skates, ice skates or skate boards*—maintaining or achieving balance in some activity. "Cheap skate"; "good skate"; "skating on thin ice" (warning of danger).

SKELETON · not developed; may be a need for more calcium in the system; a death symbol. "A skeleton in the closet"; "skeleton force"; "skeleton at the feast" (a person that brings gloom to a festive occasion).

SKIING · both water and snow skiing concern balance; on snow could indicate the spiritual balance is in a cold, hardened state, or going "down hill" fast.

SKIN · the individual's facade; *skin rash*—"rash" behavior causing trouble to surface. "Thick-skinned" (insensitive); "thin-skinned" (too sensitive); to be "skinned alive"; by the "skin of your teeth"; "no skin off your nose." "I've Got You Under My Skin."

SKIPPING · skipping something important. (See *dancing*)

SKULL & CROSSBONES · poison; death symbol; a warning that there is something or someone poisonous in your life.

SKULLCAP · a religious symbol for ideals which must be acted upon daily.

SLEET · warning of dangerous situation. (See *ice*)

SLIDING · a warning of danger; a recent misdemeanor. "Backsliding"; "going downhill."

SMILE · approval. "Smile and the world smiles with you"; "let a smile be your umbrella."

SMOKE · impending catastrophe; confusion. Biblically, smoke or a cloud sometimes symbolized God's glory or constant leadership (I

Kings 8:10–11 and Isa. 6:4). Smoking—emotionally disturbed; negative. Look at the background for clues to the meaning of the dream. "Where there's smoke there's fire"; "smoke-screen."

SNAPSHOT · (See *pictures*)

SNARL · a confused or disordered state; trouble; anger; entanglement, complication.

SNEEZE · warning of an oncoming cold; associated with allergies and the thymus center. "Nothing to sneeze at" (don't make light of).

SNOW · may mean a "cold" nature; a spiritual area needs thawing; protection (covers and protects plants during winter). "Blanket of snow"; "snowed under"; "snow job" (a cover-up or deceit); "pure as the driven snow"; to "snow-ball" (rolling down hill or accumulating rapidly). (See *ice*)

SOAP · cleansing needed or being done; be cleansed of mind and purpose. "Soft-soap"; "soap-box"; "soap opera"; "wash your mouth out with soap."

SORE · anger; something unattended to; sadness; sorrow or distress. "Sore-head"; "sore loser."

SPADE · *ace of spades*—death symbol; *shovel*—implement of work. "Dig in" (work hard); "call a spade a spade" (tell it like it is); "shovel it in" (eating).

SPEECH · *inability to speak*—not expressing oneself properly.

SPHINX · the mysterious sphinx, half human, half animal, represents people's divided instincts, with spiritual (heaven) as well as animal (earth) qualities.

SPINE · (See *back;* also *thirty-three* in Numbers chapter) "Chills run up and down my spine."

SPLINTER · a foreign object in the body often causes physical discomfort; divergent views. "Splinter off."

SPONGE · something needs to be or is being absorbed. "Sponge" (one who takes advantage of others, a parasite); "throw in the sponge."

SPOON · giving, or receiving, spiritual food. "Spoon-fed"; "born with a silver spoon in one's mouth."

SPOT · a stain on the character or reputation; reproach; blemish. "Put on the spot."

SQUARE · (See *mandala* in Archetypes chapter)

SQUEEZE · something being crushed. "Put the squeeze on"; "squeeze it until it is dry."

STAB · hostile acts or cutting remarks are inflicting wounds on self or others. "Stab in the back"; "to take a stab at."

STAGE · putting on an act; a period of growth. "Upstage"; "stage mother"; "on stage"; "stage hand."

STAR · symbol for achievement; high spiritual ideals; let your own light shine through. (See Archetypes chapter)

STATUE · honor what the statue stands for; rigid, unyielding ideas or emotions; lack of personality. Something needs to be brought to life.

STEAL/STEEL · perhaps a judgment that the dreamer is taking credit that belongs to the Creator; trying to get something for nothing. Look for the play on words (steel/stiff). "Steel yourself"; "steel-like" (color, hardness, inflexibility).

STEAM · "put steam under it"—change of vibrations from water to steam (more power added). Some emotion needs to be vented.

STOCKINGS · (See *shoes*)

STONE · (See Archetypes chapter)

STORM · stormy life; difficult time or troublesome times. To "find a safe harbor in a storm"; "storm trooper"; "storm proof"; "storm cellar." (See *tornado* and *hurricane*)

STUDY · someone or something needs more attentive consideration and research. "Study to show thyself worthy" (the most often quoted reading in the Edgar Cayce documents).

STUMBLE · a blunder; a "false step" has been taken.

SUBTERRANEAN · deeper level of the mind (subconscious). (See *cellar* and *basement* in Buildings chapter)

SUMMER · (See *seasons*)

SUN/SON · the sun without, the Son within; source of all energy in the solar system; God or religion; when the sun or any other heavenly light is obscured or extinguished, maybe some aspect of the spiritual life has been damaged. *Son* (Christ); *sun* (light); center of self (Higher Self). *Sunglasses*—seeing the world through "dark" glasses; a protection from the sun. "Sunny disposition."

SWEEPING · some area of life needs cleaning up. "A clean sweep"; "sweep it under the carpet."

SWIMMING · spiritual activity; the difficulty or ease with which one swims indicates retrogression or progression; if the swimming is difficult, the dream may be saying, "swim with the tide." "Swimming uphill"; "in the swim." (See *water* in Archetypes chapter)

SWORD · divides the true from the false, right from wrong; energy or power used constructively or destructively. (The two-edged sword has the same meaning as the single-edged sword.) "People who live by the sword, die by the sword"; "sword of justice."

· T ·

TEETH · often related to speech, although actual dental work may be indicated. *Lots of teeth*—too much talking; *Loose teeth*—loose or careless speech; *false teeth*—falsehoods, angry words; *crooked teeth*—same as for false teeth only in an uglier context; *teeth falling out*—verbosity, repeating gossip, unkind or untrue words; *braces*—need for control of words; *infected teeth*—foul language; *tooth brush*—clean up the language, *buck teeth*—forceful words that cause negative reactions. "Sink your teeth into"; "by the skin of your teeth."

TELEPHONE · message or communication coming; *ringing*—message is here.

TELEVISION · communication with pictures and speech, implying a fuller experience of the senses; a conversion may be implied since light and sound are converted into electrical waves and then reconverted into visible light rays and audible sound. "Get the picture."

THORNS · difficulties, annoyances, grievances. "Thorn in my side."

THROAT · associated with the thyroid, the fifth spiritual center, represents will power (Thy will be done). (See Spiritual Centers)

THUMB · in palmistry, the two sections of the thumb represent logic and will. "Under the thumb"; "thumbs up," sign of being in control; "thumbs down"; "rule of thumb"; "thumb-nail sketch"; "all thumbs."

THUNDER · a warning of coming trouble. "To steal one's thunder."

TIED-UP · (See *rope*)

TOMBSTONE · identification of a dead issue; possible death symbol.

TOM-TOM · primitive communication. (See *drums*)

TONGUE · related to speech. "Thick tongue"—not speaking clearly; "forked tongue"—deceit. "Tongue-in-cheek"; "tongue tied"; "on the tip of my tongue"; "to speak in tongues"; "hold your tongue"; "tongue lashing."

TOOLS · instruments for building. "Tools of one's trade" (can be applied to one's spiritual building).

TORNADO · overwrought, tormented mind; ideas that lead to destruction. (See *air* in Archetypes chapter)

TOWER · the superconscious, because it towers above all. One who "lives in an ivory tower"; "tower of strength"; "Tower of Babel."

TOYS · immaturities; to act idly without seriousness ("toy around with"); miniature of bigger things. "A plaything."

TRAP · (See *pit*)

TUNNEL · the subconscious; escaping a problem by tunneling out. "Tunnel-vision" (see things narrowly, or only one way); "light at the end of the tunnel" (hope after a difficult trial).

· U ·

UNABLE TO MOVE · (See *paralysis*)

UMBRELLA · protection. (See *rain*)

UNDERCLOTHES · things that are personally close to us; hidden ideas, habits, prejudices, attitudes.

UNIFORM · conformity; unchanging; a nurse or doctor represents the healing influence; a fireman "puts out the fire." Uniforms represent some kind of authority, usually self enforcing the laws within. (See *clothing*; also Dream Characters chapter)

URINATE · cleansing needed or being done internally.

· V ·

VACATION · rest and relaxation needed; not on the job; may be saying "take it easy."

VALENTINE · (See *heart*)

VERMIN · unclean body, mind, or spirit.

VIOLIN · high vibrations. "Nero fiddled while Rome burned"; "fiddling around"; "fiddle-dee-dee."

VISION · a conscious experience similar to the dream state (an altered state of consciousness); a fourth dimension experience; a divine or spiritual agency mainly prophetic in character, such as the Revelation.

VOLCANO · the eternal fire at the core of the earth symbolizes God, the eternal fire at our core; a warning that something may be ready to erupt. States of eruption (Washington, Hawaii), may indicate your inner state.

VOMIT · you shall pay for it (the law of compensation); a purging (something swallowed needs to be gotten out of the system). Dog eating his *vomit* (a biblical expression)—you are repeating your mistakes. "You make me sick."

· W ·

WALKING · moving ahead under one's own volition; perhaps implies exercise. "One step at a time"; "walk out"; "walk off with."

WALLET · (See purse)

WAR · conflicts within self; violent or hostile opposition to something; can be prophetic. "Warmonger."

WASHING • cleansing needed, or being done. "Don't wash your dirty laundry in public"; "all washed up"; to "wash your hands" of something.

WATER · (See Archetypes chapter)

WEB · pitfalls, snares, traps. The "web of intrigue"; "oh what a tangled web we weave, when first we practice to deceive." (See *spider*, under "Insects," in Animals chapter)

WEDDING · (See Archetypes chapter)

WEEDS · neglect of higher principles; things that need to be "weeded out" of one's life. "Rid the garden of weeds."

WELL · inward sources of life opened up by the will. "The well of living water" (John 4:10–14). (See *water* in Archetypes chapter)

WHISTLE · blowing a whistle is signal to stop; call attention to.

"Wet your whistle"; "whistling in the dark"; "whistle while you work"; "if you want me, just whistle."

WILDERNESS · a multitude of undisciplined and uncultivated thoughts; "entering into the silence" (meditation) to commune with God. The Jews spent forty years in the wilderness; according to the Edgar Cayce readings this is a period of cleansing. (See number *four* in the Numbers chapter)

WIND · refreshing new attitudes, ideas, feelings. *Strong wind*— warning of an approaching storm; often has to do with mental activities; restless mind; flightiness; to be "windy" (verbose). "An ill wind blows no good"; "the four winds"; "between the wind and the water" (vulnerable); "how the wind blows"; "take the wind out of one's sails"; "it's in the wind." (See *air*)

WINE · (See Archetypes chapter)

WINTER · (See *seasons*)

WOODS · unknown territory; the unconscious; confusion. "You're not out of the woods yet"; "babe in the woods." (See *forest*)

WOUND · possible warning about physical health; to hurt someone or oneself. "Lick your wounds."

· XYZ ·

XEROX · reproducing mistakes, referring to activity of the previous day; copying when the creative talent within could be used.

X-RAY · penetrative vision, the ability to see inside or through something. "X-ray eyes" (see inside and outside).

YARD · *backyard*—things done out of sight of the public; *frontyard*— done in public view, out in the open. (See Buildings chapter)

YEAST · to increase.

ZEALOUS · something done with enthusiasm; possibly the true meaning of "a jealous God" (zealous God), according to the George Lamsa Bible, translated from the Aramaic.

3

Dream Characters

In almost every dream, the dreamer is present and recognizable. But what about all those other characters who are usually present as well? In some cases the dream-character represents an actual person, especially someone with whom the dreamer is intimately associated or emotionally involved. However, much of the time the dream-character is an aspect of the dreamer's own personality. It is often difficult to determine whether the dream-character is actually Aunt Susie or the part of oneself that, like her, tends to talk too much. We must look at the dream from both angles and then decide which interpretation gives the most appropriate guidance to a current situation. Sometimes both approaches are helpful.

Generally, *female figures* unknown to the dreamer represent the feminine qualities, that is, emotion, affection, compassion, loyalty, passivity, sympathy; unknown *male figures* may represent the masculine qualities, such as aggression, ambition, action, assertiveness, intellect. The presence of a member of the opposite sex in a dream may suggest that the dreamer needs to incorporate more secondary sexual characteristics into his or her personality. The dual aspects of the male/female principle may be paired in a number of ways—wisdom/love, reason/intuition, mind/emotion, spirit/matter. All may at one time or another be useful in deciphering the meaning of a dream figure. However, as a rule of thumb, we suggest the dreamer start with this: *female*—the emotional, receptive, feeling side; *male*—the active, projective, thinking side.

The size of the dream-character may be important, especially if it is emphasized. A very *tall person* may be someone the dreamer sees as a "giant" in his or her life, or who "towers" over others. (Other dream contents should help decide if this is a positive or a negative view.) A very *short person* may be someone who is "small" in his or her life, who "comes up short," or doesn't "measure up." ("Small" in this context can be either someone who has little influence on the dreamer, or someone who is spiritually undeveloped.) A *fat person* to one dreamer may suggest an affluent, substantial individual, but to another, one who indulges the appetites. A *thin person* may indicate one who keeps close tabs on the appetites, or on the other hand one who is emaciated and lacks substance. (As you can see, only the dreamer can interpret his or her own symbols. All anyone else can do is offer ideas and suggestions.) As we have said, the appearance of a dream-character who is little known or a stranger to the dreamer is probably a comment on the dreamer. In this case, the sex of the image may be noteworthy. Only as a last resort should the image be considered as a wish-fulfillment. (For example, a short person dreaming of being tall.)

One of the most enigmatic occurrences in dreams is the changing of one individual into another, or the substitution of one person for another during the dream itself. For example, Jane may be playing a role and suddenly she becomes Steve. Possibly, Jane and Steve have a common characteristic which is also shared by the dreamer. If this happens, the dreamer needs to decide whether it is a desirable or an undesirable characteristic. The dream-source does not make judgments, it merely states facts. If a dream figure known to the dreamer is changed into a stranger, the dream may be saying that there is something about the person that the dreamer doesn't know. Some dream experts suggest that the "changing-into-another-person" dream experience is not actually a transformation, but that the person is, in effect, a double figure: for example, your sister *is* your friend. Also, consider the possibility that the dream may be a reminder that things, or people, *do* change.

Less frequently, a dream-character is changed into an animal. This may convey the dreamer's feelings about the person—based, of course, on how the dreamer feels about the particular animal. For instance, a dreamer changes Uncle John into a dog. If the dreamer loves dogs, then Uncle John emerges as friendly and loyal. However, if the dreamer fears dogs he or she may regard Uncle John as a threat. (Here, perhaps, the dream may also be admonishing the dreamer to stop treating Uncle John "like a dog.")

A crowd in a dream is open to various interpretations. To Freud, a crowd of anonymous people denotes a secret: something the dreamer doesn't want to reveal, or some aspect of the dreamer's personality of which only he or she is aware. Other analysts postulate that the "something hidden" is actually another person, possibly an unattainable or unacceptable love. Jung offered the idea that a dream of multitudes of people designates a universal concern and not an individual one. To many dreamers, however, the crowd represents the feeling that everyone is watching them and making judgments on them. Quite possibly, the crowd represents the dreamer watching and forming a self opinion. A group of people can also symbolize an accumulation of ideas or thoughts. It can represent the qualities of the lower self. Consider the cliché "lost in the crowd," or "one of the crowd."

Occasionally the dreamer may be presented with a scenario that seems to be from a different time period. The costumes and surroundings appear to be from another era and locale. The dreamer may want to consider the possibility of being given a clue to a past-life experience.

The absence of a person from a group closely associated with the dreamer—such as family, friends, or co-workers—may indicate an absence of the characteristic or viewpoint of the missing person. It is up to the dreamer to determine if that aspect is something that should be added to or left out of his or her life.

OCCUPATION AND HIGHER SELF CHARACTERS

Sometimes dream-characters are noteworthy because of their occupation rather than because of who they are. It is necessary, of course, to consider these figures within the context of the whole dream. The following list suggests a few of the traits associated with specific roles or occupations. Since the dreamer is the only one who can accurately interpret his or her own images, these suggestions are offered as a stimulus to the imagination.

Some of the characters which represent a measure of self-discipline can also be Higher Self symbols, such as the "policing" self, "nursing" self, "law-abiding" self. As always, however, the meaning will be dependent upon personal associations. For instance, if Dr. John Doe dreams of a doctor, the meaning may be work related.

ACTOR/ACTRESS · putting on an act; escaping the world of reality; that part of the actor/actress that is a star; may be saying of a specific person that he/she should be treated like a star.

ATHLETE · may suggest being a good sport about something, or perhaps that you are a poor sport about a situation; you may need to cooperate more with others. "It's not whether you win or lose, but how you play the game."

BOSS/EMPLOYER · you may be too "bossy"; someone may be too "bossy" in your life; dependency relationship; may be a call for assertiveness in a situation; a suggestion of power and control; or a call to be more decisive. Maybe someone is being too dependent on the dreamer.

BUTCHER · ability to "cut" someone or something; a brutal means of cutting (a butcher slaughters, unlike a surgeon who cuts to preserve life). "Cut down to size"; "cut it out."

CONSTRUCTION WORKER · doing something constructive in life, such as building; may be bringing something together.

COOK · the ability to fill a hunger; you may have done something recently that says "now you're cooking."

DETECTIVE/INVESTIGATOR · something needs investigating; may be calling attention to your over-concern with something that is none of your business.

DOCTOR/PHYSICIAN · call for a physical checkup; the doctor within may be healing an area of the mental, physical, or spiritual body. "Physician, heal thyself."

FARMER · you may be sowing and cultivating something in your life that you should become more aware of. Maybe more time needs to be spent cultivating and transforming the "earthy" (lower self) into the (heavenly) Higher Self.

FIREMAN · an emotional fire needs to be put under control (perhaps temper or lust). A play on words may indicate that you will be a "fired man." (see *fire* in Archetypes chapter)

GARDENER · the fruitful, productive area of life may need cultivating.

JUDGE · are you judging or being judged by others? You may be "handing down" decisions that you should not make. May be saying you should consult the true Judge when making a decision.

LAWYER · represents "the Law"; may be reminding you that something in your life needs to be represented, or needs counseling, or that you need to defend something. "The best defense is a good offense."

MAID/HOUSEKEEPER · since it is the duty of the maid/housekeeper to keep things tidy, clean, and in order, the dream may be saying that you need to do the same; or you may need to be of service to someone. (Look for the play on words—"made" self.)

MINISTER/PREACHER · may express the need to take care of someone, as in "ministering"; you may be "preaching" instead of "ministering."

NUN · might be saying you put too much emphasis on sex; a need to be of service to others; you may need more seclusion in order to develop the higher feelings of the spirit.

NURSE · a need to serve others or self. Something may need to be "nursed" or cared for.

POLICEMAN · some area of your life may need to be protected or "policed"; something may need to be arrested; you might be too protective in some area of your life.

PRIEST · you may need to make a confession about something or be more forgiving toward others. Like nun, may be saying you put too much emphasis on sex. A call to more service or religion.

PROSTITUTE · selling yourself in an unworthy way. In some cases it can be a form of service to humankind.

SERVANT · a call to be of service, perhaps to the "Master, whom I have chosen to serve."

SOLDIER · may be calling for more discipline in your life. Soldiers are also known for bravery, so may be saying that you should be a brave "soldier" in some area of your life; perhaps you were brave in a situation that day.

TEACHER/PROFESSOR · look for the learning situation in your life. You may have taught someone a lesson. You might be going through a testing period of your life. Are you professing to know everything?

Several of these dream-characters are obvious authority figures. Since they represent people in command of a particular situation, the dreamer can assume that they speak with the "voice of authority" and should be listened to. However, the mere appearance of the dream-figure probably does not tell the whole story. What is the character doing? Who is playing the role—oneself? an acquaintance? a stranger? These things must also be considered before arriving at a final interpretation.

Other dream-figures may be personifications of the Higher Self, the conscience and its dictates. This Higher Self occasionally appears in dreams, telling how it sees the dreamer and indicating how the dreamer should act. Jesus, Moses, Mohammed, Buddha, the Virgin Mary or other spiritual figures in a dream are probably Higher Self symbols, suggesting that the dreamer incorporate into his or her life the attitudes of that dream-character. An authority figure is frequently also a Higher Self image. In the dreams of a woman, this self often manifests itself as a superior female figure, a *priestess, queen, noblewoman, wise old-woman*. In a man, it may appear as a superior masculine figure, a *guru, king, prince, wise old man*. (See *Anima/Animus* in Archetypes chapter)

UNDESIRABLE CHARACTERS

Most dreamers have no problem in identifying with, say, "Officer Friendly," the neighborhood cop, or "Nurse Jane," the lady dressed in pure white. Most certainly, they can identify with Queen Guinevere or Sir Lancelot. But what of all those nefarious or terrifying figures that intrude upon the dreamers in their "unconscious" states? Many dreamers have tried to preserve their unblemished image of themselves by saying, "But it wasn't *me* that chopped off all those heads! It was the Queen of Hearts!" Or, "What characteristic could I possibly share with ne'er-do-well cousin Harley"?

Unfortunately, all the unsavory, unpleasant dream-characters are also the dreamer's own creations, representing characteristics that he or she would rather not claim. Usually, they are one's "ugly" and frightening inner feelings, desires, and fears. Some light may be shed on these "dark" figures if the dreamer questions them, just as with the more benign creations.

CONVICT/PRISONER · an indication of restrictions and perhaps a desire to be free; maybe anti-social tendencies and energies that need to be "put away." Ask yourself "Have I imprisoned some of my feelings; am I being warned about recriminations?"

DEVILS/DEMONS · Am I being warned of "sinful" actions or thoughts? ("Get thee behind me, Satan!") The "good or evil" conflicts within self: the devil as an embodiment of the personal will as opposed to Divine will. (See Archetypes chapter)

GANGSTERS · a warning that negative attitudes could be "ganging" up and threatening to get out of hand; emotional tensions; are you traveling with the "wrong gang"?

GHOSTS · thoughts that have no form or substance; being "haunted" by things of the past; something may need to be put aside because there is "not a ghost of a chance." Something may be "spooky."

GIANT · you may be a "giant" in your field, or may become a giant in something you are about to undertake; someone that "towers" over others.

MONSTER · thoughts or actions could be "monstrous"; examine self for negative traits, such as bad temper, jealousy, or cruelty. "Green-eyed monster" (jealousy).

PRIMITIVE PEOPLE/SAVAGES · uncivilized or uncouth behavior, speech, or attitudes. May be a call to work on the higher evolution of self.

THIEF/ROBBER · perhaps an intrusion that comes upon you like a "thief in the night"; a warning that your values may be threatened. "No honor among thieves"—is someone out to "rob" you of your ideals?

WITCH · look for a play on the word *which:* which way should I go? An undesirable characteristic needs to be corrected. Good witches may be indicated by the background of the dream. "Witch hunt"; "witchcraft"; "witchdoctor."

It is worth repeating that a dream figure may be less important than what is taking place in the dream, or than the emotions experienced in the dream. Also, the dreamer's feelings upon awakening are significant. No matter how frightening the dream, the first step toward wholeness is self-awareness and attunement with the inner, more spiritualized self. Negative attitudes and qualities must be recognized so that they can be integrated by the Higher Self and changed into positive, constructive qualities.

FAMILY MEMBERS

O f all the dream-characters met in dreams, the ones most likely to be playing themselves are family members. First, then, one must consider dream-relatives in the context of the whole dream. If they seem not to be their actual selves, and the dream is not saying that their most outstanding trait can also be found in the dreamer, then the following suggestions may be helpful. We are, of course, here considering stereotype figures, who will not necessarily mirror the qualities of the actual person.

ANCESTORS · preceding stages of soul growth.

FATHER · old attitudes, especially if the dreamer is male; the providing side of self; the counseling side; the decision-making side; authority or Higher Self symbol. (See Archetypes chapter)

GRANDPARENT · old attitudes; desire to be pampered; authority or Higher Self symbol; "grand parent."

HUSBAND · the mind (male) in alliance with the emotions (female); the masculine side of self (logical, active, intellectual, forceful); the provider, protector, the manager, life's companion. Review the relationship with the spouse—loving and communicative, or disagreeable and selfish? "Head of the household."

HUSBAND & WIFE · the mental and emotional natures united and productive of thoughts and actions (children).

MOTHER · if the dreamer is female, may be old attitudes; the nurturing side of self; the protective side; the creative side; the inborn, innate nature; authority or Higher Self symbol. (See Archetypes chapter)

OFFSPRING · (See *child* in next section)

SIBLING · the supportive side; related aspects having the same source; review the relationship for indications of "sibling rivalry." "I *am* my brother's keeper."

WIFE · the emotions (female) balanced with the mind (male); the feminine side of self (emotional, intuitive, receptive, gentle); the supportive nature; the balancer, nurturer; the dependable side; life's companion. As with *husband*, review the relationship with the spouse—loving and communicative, or disagreeable and selfish?

OTHER DREAM-CHARACTERS

BABY · something new as a result of a union of mind and emotions, wisdom and love; new important cycle; feeling of helplessness. The dream baby who is beautiful, wise-looking, and able to speak means new consciousness, the rebirth of the lower self to higher and nobler ideals or bright new ideas. *Girl baby*—new birth of feminine traits (feelings and emotions); *boy baby*—new birth of masculine traits (activities or intellectual pursuits); *adopted baby*—dreamer may be taking responsibility or credit for something he or she did not conceive and incubate; dream may be saying adopt some new ideas; *twin babies*—a "doubled" idea (especially important); "double-duty" required in some area; *deformed baby*—ill-conceived idea; *sick baby*—failure to overcome obstacles; *nursing a baby*—feeding and nourishing ideals; *dropping a baby*—"dropping" or neglect of higher ideals. To "act like a baby"; "babe in the woods" (vulnerable).

BLIND PERSON · not facing facts; lack of spiritual perception; blind to an idea. "The blind leading the blind"; "blind spot."

CHILD · undeveloped self; immature self; helpful beginnings needing further aid from the dreamer; feelings of inferiority; desire to shirk responsibilities; inner child-like qualities; fun-loving self. Two significant qualities of a child are forgiveness and trust. "For a little child shall lead them"; "unless ye become as a child, ye shall not enter the kingdom of heaven."

CLOWN · fun-loving aspect; a need or desire to disguise sadness. "Making a clown out of yourself"; "clown around."

DEAF/DUMB PERSON · inability to hear, recognize, or express the Truth.

DECEASED PEOPLE · if known persons, the quality associated with them is dead in you; dead issues; a need to resurrect something that is "dead"; a communication from a soul (the image of a deceased loved one sometimes appears to offer love and encouragement in a time of trial).

DEFORMED PEOPLE · some aspect of self has not been properly developed. (Consider the specific part of the body for further insights; for example, a deformed foot may mean a "twisted" understanding.)

DWARF · the lower self which is small in comparison to the Higher Self; stunted growth.

FAMOUS PEOPLE · hero/heroine image; an outstanding trait or deed associated with a specific individual. The names themselves may be used as a pun. Richard *Widmark* could suggest "wide of the mark"; Henry *Fonda*—"fond of"; *Hedy* Lamarr—too much head (intellectual); *Eartha* Kitt—earthy; Harry *Truman*—a true man. Any proper name may be used in the same way.

FOREIGNERS · alien thoughts or ideas; those tendencies of our personality we have not lived, good or bad; unconscious aspects of self. (See *shadow* in Archetypes chapter; also *black* in Color chapter)

GYPSIES · instinctual wisdom; free-spirited aspect; desire to wander.

KING/QUEEN · power and wealth; highest spiritual force; overcoming the self's animal nature; self-mastery. "Fit for a king"; "live like a king"; "queen bee."

NEIGHBOR · a quality with a close affinity to another quality. "Love thy neighbor as thyself."

OLD MAN/OLD WOMAN · old habits or attitudes; authority or Higher Self figure. (See Archetypes chapter)

ORPHAN · developing aspect deprived of guidance and nurturing.

SLAVE · the lower nature enslaved by its passions and desires. Are you enslaved to someone?

TWINS · if the person who appears as twins is known to the dreamer, some trait, viewpoint, or values of that person may need to be "duplicated," or made twice as strong, within the dreamer; may also be a trait that has been over-emphasized, either in the dreamer or in the person dreamed about; an issue that has two sides to it. (See *baby*)

VIRGIN · unfulfilled emotional side, requiring a union with the rational side to become whole; the purified emotions uninfluenced by the desire-mind (male). The *virgin birth* implies that the body is in perfect balance to conceive with the Holy Spirit.

WIDOW · love or emotions deprived of wisdom or logic.

WIDOWER · wisdom or intellect deprived of emotion or love.

WIZARD/SORCERER ·   the lower self which is attracted to impractical or false ideas.

YOUNG BOY / YOUNG MAN ·   immature thinking or actions; undeveloped male aspects (reason, intellect, logic, etc.).

YOUNG GIRL / YOUNG WOMAN ·   immature emotions; undeveloped female aspects (love, feelings, receptivity, etc.).

4

Vehicles

Vehicles usually represent the body. Many factors are relevant to interpreting dreams of vehicles. For example, is the dreamer alone, with others, in the back seat, on the passenger side? Is the dreamer traveling independently or with others, by his or her own efforts or someone else's? Is the dreamer at the wheel and in control? Is the journey uphill and downhill, smooth or rough? Is it along a road, path, railway, across a sea, or through the sky? What is the method of travel? Consider the following suggestions, keeping in mind that a personal association may change the meaning.

AIRPLANE · elevated approach to goals; a swift and easy journey toward a goal without much concern for details on the way; high ideals. May be saying "rise above the situation," or the opposite, "get down to earth." *Jet plane*—traveling fast with high ideals; *airplane crash*—loss of hopes, ambitions, or high ideals; loss of control in some area, warning of disaster.

AMBULANCE · warning of emergency situation; help is on the way.

AUTOMOBILE · the physical body, the vehicle used through this life; movement toward a goal or away from a situation. *Driving* *your own car*—in control of life; *driving backward*—going backward in life; *being a passenger*—a passive individual being controlled by someone or something else ("going along for the ride"); *being in the backseat*—taking a backseat in life ("backseat driver"); *windshield wipers*—getting a clearer view in a stormy situation; *tires*—foundations; "spinning your wheels"; "tired"; *flat tire*—look for physical imbalance or injury; how many tires are flat relates to the severity of the condition; *headlights*—sight, insight, perception; take a look at the situation; *headlights out*—loss of consciousness, or awareness; *brakes*—use of the will; *low-powered, small car*—low energy; *big, luxurious car*—be careful of paying too high a price physically, for indulging the appetites; high-powered; *running out of gas*—lack of energy. Any dream involving a car with mechanical trouble should first be checked for a literal interpretation.

BICYCLE · achieving balance, physically, mentally, spiritually. Look for balance in the situation indicated by dream.

BOAT · voyage of life, with a broader view of the individual's life than land travel; a boat is the vehicle that takes the dreamer over the depths of the unconscious. *Speed boat*—skimming over the surface of the unconscious; *missing a boat*—failure to grasp the deeper implications of events; *disembarking*—the end of an experience, returning home; *drifting helplessly*—drifting through life without a purpose.

BUS · overweight problem; on a journey with others; a limited view of life's events.

CARRIAGE · *horse and carriage*—romance; *baby carriage*—immaturity; vehicle for a new way of life.

DIRIGIBLE · buoyant state of mind; overweight problem ("blimp").

FIRE ENGINE · a need to fight out-of-control emotions; the resources are available to fight out-of-control emotions.

HEARSE · possible death symbol; a dead issue needs to be carried away.

MOTORCYCLE · traveling fast, but with balance.

RAFT · a makeshift, unstable vehicle for traveling over the depths of the unconscious.

TRAIN · on a journey with others and possibly a powerful trip; high-powered personality; fast life-style; the course is set, so don't get off the main track. *Train station*—anticipating a change or meeting someone. "Train of thought"; "side-tracked."

TRUCK · associated with work; overweight; carrying a heavy load. *Rickety truck*—poor health or work habits; *garbage truck*—get rid of the "garbage" in your life; *pick-up truck*—a casual, informal manner; quick energy available, or needed.

5

Buildings

Dream-structures are states of consciousness that we have built for ourselves. Our actions in dreams indicate what is presently going on in our lives and what we are in the process of building; structures indicate something finished, something already built. The type of structure should give the dreamer a clue as to what area of life is being considered: a hospital has to do with health, a courthouse with justice, a school with learning. As with any symbol, a personal association may change the meaning. A dream of being in school probably will not have the same interpretation for a teacher as it will for an engineer.

A house, often representing our everyday state of consciousness, is the most common structure found in dreams; it is where the soul lives while on earth. Notice the condition of the house: is it in good condition, indicating a positive and healthy mental state, or is it run-down and in need of repair? Is it an old house, reminiscent of past times and old ways of thinking, or is it a new house, suggesting that the dreamer may be looking at things in a new way? Pay attention to the furnishings, which may be saying something about the thoughts occupying our "house." Are the rooms appropriately furnished? Sparsely furnished? Are they neat and tidy, or are they cluttered, perhaps giving the dreamer insights into the organization of his or her mental activities. Is the lot on which the house is built spacious or adequate or small? In other words, is there space to grow and expand in consciousness? Is the house in a city where there is lots of activity, or is it in a tranquil, rural setting? The dreamer must decide, based on other contents and feelings in the dream, if the dream is saying that he or she needs a lot of mental stimulation (city) or more time for meditation and reflection (rural).

The size of the structure may be significant: that is, whether it is large and impressive looking, or small and confining. Does it have a good foundation, a solid base? Consider things like shape, surface features, construction material, landscaping. If there are other people in the building, the dream may be drawing attention to relationships or activities involving those people. If others are not present, it may represent conditions within the dreamer himself. For example, a dream of sitting all alone in an auditorium (related to hearing) may be telling the dreamer to listen to what others say. The ideas in the following alphabetized list are only suggestions; remember that your own definition of the symbols, based on your own personal references, may be different.

AIRPORT · often associated with high ideals or religious endeavors; soul trip; a desire to rise above worldly problems or responsibilities.

APARTMENT · temporary state of affairs; no return on the investment; no room for expansion; living with consideration of others (other families are involved in apartment living). Since an apartment is part of a larger building, it may be related to the development of only one aspect of the dreamer's whole life.

BANK · where "treasures" are stored; material security. A *deposit*—to add to one's assets; a *withdrawal*—to call upon one's assets. "You can bank on that."

BARN · associated with labor. Since this is a home for domestic animals, and a storage place for farm implements, grain, and other essentials, the dream may be implying that each individual has a large inner storage place containing the essentials for inner growth.

BEAUTY PARLOR/BARBER SHOP · thoughts are cleansed, created, or rearranged; new ideas.

BOARDING HOUSE · essentials are provided, but payment is required.

CASTLE · strength and power; security; elegant living; living in a fantasy world. "Castle in the sky."

CHURCH · spiritual state; God within; a place of peace and refuge; a place of sanctuary; possibly the mother (Mother Church), or the Self; place of baptism, therefore of rebirth.

CLEANERS · clean up some aspect of the personality (clothes). "Taken to the cleaners."

COURTHOUSE · feelings of being judged; justice being served; may relate to courtship.

FIREHOUSE · contains what is necessary to extinguish a fire (anger, uncontrolled passions).

FUNERAL PARLOR · something dead needs to be laid to rest; something dead needs to be (re)viewed. "It's your funeral."

HOSPITAL · a place of healing—physical, mental, emotional; birth and death.

HOTEL · transitory or temporary situation or mental state; travel.

HOUSE · The exterior of the house may represent the body; the interior, the mind and its different levels. The lower levels of a house generally refer to the subconscious mind, the ground level to the conscious, and the upper levels to the superconscious.

Old, rickety house—a body, or a state of consciousness, in need of repair; *unfinished house*—lack of love, gentleness, understanding, or order; *flooded house*—health problem (too much fluid in the body); emotions (water) out of control; *large house*—desire or need for a more expansive way of life; *small house*—desire or need for a more restricted way of life; dreamer's *childhood house*—old physical, mental, or emotional state; a regressive fantasy to evade current problems; *repairing a house*—working on rifts within self or family. *Fence* or *wall*—separation of self and others; obstacles, barriers, dividers; confinement, privacy; "on the fence"; "don't fence me in"; "mend one's fences"; feeling "fenced in."

Front yard—front of the mind; the "front" you present; "out in front"; "up front"; "out in the open"; *back yard*—in the back of the mind, hidden from public view (inner consciousness); privacy; unpleasant pursuits; "background" (something little seen or noticed).

Porch—extension of inner self; outside of self; insecurity; *tower*—superconscious (it "towers" over all); *garage*—protection, contains "tools" for maintenance and repairs; *fire escape*—a way out of an inflammable frame of mind; *windows*—perception; seeing both sides; the "eyes of the soul"; *curtains*—perception obscured; privacy; *black curtains*—possible death symbol; *white curtains*—possible death symbol to one unafraid of dying; "curtains" (death—as at the end of a play); *roof*—ideals (the highest point); protection; *falling off a roof*—warning of a spiritual or physical "fall."

Many beautiful rooms—a growing state of consciousness; seeking beauty of character; *empty room*—lack of spiritual or mental development (furnish that room or rooms); *beautiful furnishings*—beauty of spiritual life; *rearranging furniture*—rearranging viewpoint; no direction; no anchor; *great disorder*—"set thine house in order"; *going into the next room or leaving a room*—entering a new level of consciousness or a possible death symbol; *wandering from room to room*—the process of looking within.

An *open door*—new opportunities, new cycle; pineal gland (sixth spiritual center; see Spiritual Centers chart); an opening to a new understanding and awareness; a transition; *locking or barring a door*—desire or need to lock out unpleasant conditions; not being open to new ideas or opportunities; *escaping by another door*—a way out, a means of escape; *opening front door*—receiving spiritual help; *back door*—something not in the open, usually negative or hidden; *closed door*—opportunities or activities that should not be pursued at this time; *refuse, dirt, feces, or rats at one's door*—"sin lieth at thy door"; negative attitudes which close out people and help.

Floors—support or foundations of the body, mind, and spirit; *slanted floors or walks*—slanted views; *rotting floors*—poor physical or spiritual foundation; *sinking floor*—falling away from proper ideals or principles (a sinking kitchen or dining room floor could indicate poor nutritional habits).

Ceiling—mental heights; limits; *stairs*—a way to "ascend" or "descend"; "one step at a time"; *going up stairs*—reaching for a higher consciousness; *going down stairs*—delving into the subconscious; "backstairs" (secret, underhanded); *hallways*—transitions; going from one idea to the next; change.

Underground rooms or passageways—the deep, subconscious levels of the mind; *basement or cellar*—subconscious mind; *valuables stored or buried below ground level*—subliminal abilities or ideas that need to be brought up and used; *basement playroom*—take a playful or joyful attitude toward life; *basement laundry room*—cleansing of the baser attitudes and emotions; *basement workshop*—work being done to repair or change the baser emotions and attitudes; *dark basement*—good basics, but little in-depth probing; *root cellar*—inner storehouse of "nourishment."

Beautiful ground floor—good daily activities; *kitchen*—place of preparation for physical, mental, or spiritual nourishment; *dining room*—serving or eating spiritual, mental, or physical food; *living room*—the scene for daily activities or where the living is done; *family room or playroom*—relaxation, fun, joy; *fireplace*—comfort; purification; *den or study*—work area, research, learning; *closet*— inner self; closed off; separated; desire to hide something; "secret place of the Most High" (meditation); "skeleton in the closet"; "closet-queen"; *beautiful upper floor*—a good mind, properly oriented; *bedroom*—intimate activities; rest, recuperation; "take it easy"; "sleep on it."

Bathroom—physical, mental, and spiritual cleansing going on, or to be done; *bathtub*—external cleansing needed or being done; *bathtub overflowing*—emotions out of control; *toilet bowl*—internal cleansing needed or being done; *toilet bowl overflowing*—bowels stopped up; the way needs to be made clear for eliminating impurities in life.

Attic—storehouse for the conscious mind; storage place for forgotten or neglected treasures.

JAIL · restriction; confinement; guilt feelings; *escaping from jail or prison*—a desire or need for improved conditions. "Caged in"; "behind the walls."

LIBRARY · storehouse of knowledge; search for Truth; research; house of learning and study.

MOTEL · (See *hotel*)

MUSEUM · a place to (re)view things from the past.

OFFICE · related to work, accomplishment; home away from home. "Office wife."

POLICE STATION · protection; contains the qualities capable of "arresting" those aspects that break the law.

PRISON · (See *jail*)

RAILROAD STATION · travel, change; waiting to get on the right track in life's journey.

RESTAURANT · nourishment is provided, but payment is required. The type of restaurant is important. In a fast food place or cafeteria the dreamer is required to do much to help; in an elegant setting more of the basic needs are provided, but more is expected in return.

SCHOOL · lessons to be learned; more growth is required; associated with one's school days; *schools of higher learning*—raise the thinking to a higher degree. "The old or the new school."

SERVICE STATION · re-energize the body (car) physically, mentally, or spiritually. You may need a physical check-up.

SHACK · poor dwelling place; crudely built and crudely furnished. "Shacking up."

STORE · *book store*—learning, study, research; *clothing store*—shopping for a new means of expression, or new personality; *department store*—temptation (we are tempted to spend our "valuables"); where we have choices; *drugstore*—"healing" prescriptions; abuse of drugs or medication; *health food store*—stricter, healthier diet; *old-fashioned grocery store*—inadequate nourishment; *music store*—harmony; lyrical expression; *supermarket*—eating habits, diet; *variety store*—making choices of smaller items than in a department store.

TEMPLE · spirituality. Jesus said, "Destroy this temple and in three days I will raise it up" (John 2:19). Few people thought then that he was talking about the body, but when he was crucified, he did raise his body in three days. The "temple of the Holy Ghost."

6

Animals

AQUATIC LIFE

At the highest level, aquatic life represents seeking the spiritual life. In dreams the meaning will change in accordance with surrounding symbols: muddy water, turbulent water, deep, clear water, swift-running water, etc. Things relating to the depth of the mind are usually symbolized by water and its inhabitants. Water can also symbolize transformation, for example, of a tadpole to a frog and ultimately to "Prince Charming," as the fairy tales relate.

The habitat of the life form may be helpful in deciphering the message in a dream. For instance, since a turtle lives on land and in water, a dream that includes this species may be a commentary on both the spiritual and the material life. Fish are exclusively aquatic, and dreams about them probably deal only with spiritual efforts. If the dream fish is identifiable as a particular species, consider the feeding habits of that species. Catching a bull-head could possibly be a criticism on the attitudes of the dreamer (bull-headed). However, the bull-head is a scavenger, feeding on scraps and impurities, so the dream may be suggesting that the dreamer "feed" his or her spiritual life on fresh, more substantial food, rather than on "leftovers." Other forms of aquatic life, such as the crab, will feed on their own species. A dream that includes one of these cannibalistic creatures may be a warning that someone is "devouring" the dreamer, or that the dreamer may be engaged in self-destructive activities or thinking.

As with any dream symbol, the meaning may be entirely different if there is a personal association. Dreaming of fish takes on another interpretation if the dreamer is an angler or a proprietor of a fish market. For those with no personal reference, we hope the preceding and following ideas will provide clues to their dreams involving aquatic life.

ALLIGATOR · vicious speech; destructive emotions lying in wait. (See *crocodile*)

CLAM · to be quiet. "Clam up"; "happy as a clam"; "clammy."

CRAB · third sign of the Zodiac (Cancer); a scavenger; known for traveling sideways; *claws*—the power to wound. "Crabby" (ill-natured person).

CROCODILE · cruel, vicious, thick-skinned, malicious. Since these animals are known for their ugly mouths, cruel teeth, and dangerous tails, examine recent conduct for signs of vicious speech which may have been destructive. "Crocodile tears." (See *alligator*)

EEL · slippery, base (debasing self).

FISH · twelfth sign of the Zodiac (Pisces); the Christ within. The size, color, and looks of a fish often represent the dreamer's present spiritual evolution, as does the size of the body of water (oceans, sea, lake, river, well, swimming pools, or any body of water). *Fishing*—the search for a higher consciousness (hooking the unknown, the spiritual side of life); keeping the conscious mind firmly anchored to tangible reality (earth) while trying to catch the treasures of the unconscious (depth); *catching a beautiful, large fish*—growth of the Divine Self; but if the fish is too big to land, the fisherman becomes the victim of his catch; *fishing from a boat*—uncertainty. *Eating fish*—the power of renewal, rebirth; a miraculous food, as represented by Christ feeding the five thousand. People who are referred to as "poor fish," "odd fish," or a "fish out of water" often have some inability to relate to others, possibly because of a lack of sexual attractiveness or emotional warmth. *Catfish*—"cattiness," or a weakness of spirit (they have few bones); *fish eyes*—perpetual attention because they never shut their eyes; *ugly fish*—spiritual weakness. Being eaten or swallowed by a fish, as Jonah in biblical times, can mean being swallowed by the unconscious. "Fish wife" (an abusive, vulgar woman); to be "hooked" on something; "fish or cut bait"; "drink like a fish"; "fish for" (try to get something indiscreetly); "other fish to fry (or catch)"; "fish story"; "fishy" (questionable).

FROGS · transformation (tadpole, frog, "Prince Charming"); uncleanliness; unintelligible or ugly speech; related to throat area; "frog in the throat."

JELLYFISH · no "backbone."

OCTOPUS · clinging, possessive. "All hands."

OYSTER · withdrawn; housing for a "pearl." "The world is his oyster."

SHARK · unscrupulous; voracious; a predator (takes advantage of others); someone who excels in a field. "Shark" (a greedy, artful person).

STARFISH · a "star" in spiritual life (excellence); cannibalistic.

TURTLE · withdrawn (if head is in); slow to move; carries around a protective "shell." Associated with antiquity. (See *tortoise* under "Terrestrial Life")

WHALE · excess weight; *being swallowed by a whale*, like Jonah—being swallowed by the unconscious. Look for play on word "wail." "Whale of a story."

BIRDS AND FOWL

Air is the element associated with the mind and mental activities. So it is easy to see why birds, the masters of the air, are often related to our "flights of fancy," our aspiring thoughts, ideas, hopes, and emotions. Their ability to break free of the earth correlates with people's ability to use their nobler qualities and lift their lower, material nature (earth) to a higher, more spiritual nature (sky or heaven). Carl Jung viewed these heavenly creatures as the most fitting symbol of transcendence.

According to Edgar Cayce, birds—especially the eagle—are associated with the fourth spiritual center (the thymus), which is related to love. This center is frequently referred to as the love center. Looking at birds in this way, we can understand why our dream source will sometimes use birds to symbolize the sexual act. The kind of bird, its activities, and the rest of the dream will help determine whether or not the dreamer is using this expression of love in an uplifting way.

Jung also associated birds with emotional love in some dreams. In this regard shooting birds in a dream may be a positive symbol if it means shooting down emotional love, to replace it with unconditional, universal love. To dream of a bird in a cage probably means that some "love in your life" needs to be set free. Conversely, depending on the context of the dream, it could mean an uncontrolled emotion needs to be "caged up." To dream of a bird in your house may be an idea, thought, or emotion that is enclosed within the mind (house) and needs to be released.

There are many clichés pertinent to birds. For example, "he's a bird"; "a bird in the hand is worth two in the bush"; "eat like a bird"; "birds of a feather flock together"; "for the birds"; "the birds and the bees"; "bird-brain"; "bird of ill omen"; "bird's-eye view." If a fowl is presented in a dream, look for a play on the word "foul."

Each species has its own unique characteristic, some of which are mentioned in the alphabetized list that follows. If none of these ideas seem relevant, consider the classification of the bird if possible: predatory bird, song bird, water bird, garden bird, flightless bird, caged bird. Other symbols and actions in the dream will add to your understanding of the dream bird. Remember, again, that any personal experience always takes precedence.

BLUEBIRD · happiness, joy. "Bluebird of happiness."

BLUE JAY · cunning, inquisitive, noisy; a mimic, full of mischief.

CARDINAL · graceful, flamboyant, accomplished vocalist, affectionate (the male bird cracks the sunflower seed for the female and feeds her while she incubates the eggs). A cardinal is rarely seen without its mate. Consider a reference to a high official in the church.

CATBIRD · a mimic; a good neighbor who cares for orphaned young of other species and responds quickly to a cry of distress from another bird. People also consider them good neighbors, for their playful ways and entertaining mimicry.

CHICKEN · timidity, lack of courage. "Chicken" means afraid (they rarely take their own part if confronted). "Chicken with its head cut off" (person acting lost); "chicken feed" (small change); "chicken-hearted"; "don't count your chickens before they hatch."

CROW · intelligent (they're known to play tricks on animals just for the fun of it); harsh, boastful. "Something to crow about"; "crow's feet"; "old crow"; "as the crow flies."

DOVE · messenger of peace, as the dove with the olive branch for Noah; an inner initiation, as the descent of the Holy Spirit; love ("billing and cooing"); *cooing dove or pigeon*—to speak with a soft murmur, fondly.

DUCK · since a duck is at home in the water or on land, the dream may be trying to blend the physical (earth) with the spiritual (water). To "duck" an issue.

EAGLE · official emblem of the United States, represents American independence. Archetypal symbol for the fourth spiritual center (thymus), relating to love; spiritual heights; mental activity; a person breaking free of the earth, as when the eagle soars.

FALCON · preys on others; takes advantage of others.

GOOSE · foolish actions; a simpleton. "Your goose is cooked"; "silly goose."

HAWK · grasping nature; swindler, cheater. "Hawkish" (advocate of open hostilities); "hawks and doves"; "watch like a hawk."

HUMMINGBIRD · unsurpassed maneuverability; tremendous energy; master at extracting nectar.

LARK · happiness; song of good cheer. "Happy as a lark"; "it's a lark" (pleasure).

MOCKINGBIRD · master of mockery; may suggest that the dreamer show a wider appreciation of life and expand the use of talents.

OWL · often a warning to use more judgment in affairs of the heart. "Wise old owl"; "wise as an owl"; "night owl" (a person of nocturnal habits); "night life."

PARAKEET · the "love bird," could denote a relationship of love that is caged in and needs to be freed.

PARROT · an imitator. To "parrot" (to repeat by rote).

PHOENIX · happiness and good fortune; reincarnation, because it rises to new life from its own ashes; harbinger of spiritual rebirth.

RAVEN · a symbol of wilderness; could be a reminder of God's love and the ability of God to meet all emergencies (Elijah was fed by ravens). To an Englishman, the raven might mean self-survival or survival of the British Empire; to one familiar with Edgar Allan Poe's "The Raven," it could symbolize fatalism and despair. It could also be a play on words like "raving mad."

ROBIN · traditional harbinger of spring (a new beginning or a new love).

STORK · a bearer of new life.

SWAN · beautiful life, graciousness, and beauty. "Swan song" (from the myth that swans sing sweetly just before dying).

TURKEY · Thanksgiving (perhaps a reminder to give thanks for something in your life); lack of intelligence (they sometimes drown because they don't have sense enough to come in out of the rain). "She's a turkey."

VULTURE · indiscriminate eating; greedy person who preys on others.

WREN · a combination of timidity, curiosity, and aggression. According to a Cherokee Indian myth, the wren is a busybody, flitting about learning everybody's business and reporting it to the bird's council. A sign of spring. "Song of a wren" (known for warbling).

INSECTS

Insects in a dream will often represent irritations, something that bothers or "bugs" the dreamer. They often symbolize self-reproach or the "pangs of conscience," which also "pricks." "Pests" is one of our favorite names for insects. They annoy us, bite us, infect us with diseases. They attack our crops, invade our homes, eat our food, and damage our property. When a specific kind of insect is present in a dream, think about these characteristics and how they can relate to a present experience or condition, mental or physical.

Consider, too, the type of insect. If it is a stinging variety, pay attention to the nature of the sting: some are merely annoying, some are deadly. If it is a chewing insect, such as a grasshopper or termite, are we "chewing out" ouselves or others? Or are we "chewing" (ruminating) on something constructive? Flying insects are of the air (mind) and may represent negative thoughts. Since crawling insects are of the ground, or earth (body), maybe they are related to physical problems or the earthy, material aspects. Regardless of the variety, it may be comforting to remember that most insects have a very short life span.

ANTS · annoying problems; success in a project (ants are known for their organization and work capabilities); foresight (they store up supplies for the winter). "Ants in your pants" (restless); "antsy" (anxious).

BEES · hard work and its enjoyment (honey); constructive labor; wisdom, for as the bee extracts pollen from the flowers, so may we extract wisdom from the experiences of daily life. *Bee stings*—unpleasant experiences of life; *bumble bee*—"bumbling" things; *honey bee*—"honey of a bee" (predigested food). "The birds and the bees"; "a bee in your bonnet."

BEETLES · irritations; *scarab*—sacred beetle of Egypt, symbolizing immortality of the soul.

BUTTERFLY · the unfolded, enlightened soul emerging from the confines of the baser nature; immortality; pleasure. "Butterflies, like love, go wherever they please and please wherever they go"; "butterflies in the stomach."

CATERPILLAR · destruction or disintegration; under this lowly, creeping, earthly aspect is concealed the beautiful butterfly-form.

COCKROACH · irritations hard to get rid of; carrier of dis-ease.

FLY · annoyance; carrier of dis-ease. "A fly in the ointment."

GNATS · a disturbed nervous system.

GRASSHOPPER · annoyances that may be destructive to growth.

HORNET · unpleasant experiences. "Don't stir up a hornet's nest"; "mad as a hornet."

LICE · uncleanliness of body, mind, spirit.

MOTH · secret wisdom, because they are hard to discover and are concealed by the darkness (ignorance); the dark, sinister aspect of the psyche; may be saying draw to the light, as the moth is drawn to the light. "Moth-eaten" (worn-out).

SCORPION · eighth sign of the Zodiac. Sometimes represents the "stinging" aftermath of an unfortunate experience: a warning that some activity is inflicting injury only on self; backbiting (a scorpion will sometimes sting itself with its own tail); selfishness. "Sting of death."

SPIDER · since the spider distinguishes itself by the web it builds to trap other insects; it usually symbolizes a web or trap into which the dreamer is falling. This may be a recent indiscretion, a coming temptation, a bad habit, or a warning regarding a bad business venture. Some consider the spider as the feminine figure whose affection is devouring. *Black widow*—devouring female; poisonous. "Caught in the web" (hopelessness).

TERMITE · annoyances or irritations that may be destructive to the foundations.

WORM · destruction or disintegration. When they appear in food, look for a warning against that particular food, or the diet in general. *Inch worm*—possible reference to something that needs to be taken in small doses. A "worm" (a contemptible person); "worming your way out"; "squirming like a worm"; the "worm of conscience" (something that gnaws at one inwardly); "worm's-eye view"; "the worm will turn."

TERRESTRIAL LIFE

The biblical account of Noah's taking pairs of all the animals aboard the Ark to preserve them is emblematic of the preservation of our animal instincts within. The significance of his taking pairs—one of each sex—is that these animalistic qualities are to be transcended, not destroyed. In line with this approach, animals stand for transformation in that we can learn to transform these animal instincts, so carefully preserved within, to our Divine potential.

Generally, animals represent the physical, lower nature of human life. Wild animals usually symbolize emotions or desires which are out of control, the undisciplined qualities. The wilder the animal, the more meaningful the dream in terms of primitive emotions. These symbols can be very helpful because they may give clues to hidden animosities, anger, aggression, or vengeance. Tamed, domesticated animals may represent the disciplined qualities that can be helpful in developing the Higher Self. They may also indicate that the dream involves the "domestic" life. Because they have no footing (feet), crawling animals could show spiritual progress, implying the "death" of animal instinct within.

In deciphering the meaning of an animal symbol, take into consideration the characteristics of the animal species itself. Again, any personal experience or association involving the kind of animal always takes precedence.

APE · someone who imitates. "Go ape." (See *gorilla, monkey*)

BEAR · overprotectiveness, because bears protect their offspring for two years; playfulness which can be dangerous; negative emotions or desires that crush and stifle efforts. *Three bears* (mother, father, child)—three stages of growth (feminine, masculine, immature qualities). Look for play on word "bare," such as "bare facts." "Overbearing"; "grumpy as a bear"; "hungry as a bear"; "bear-hug"; "bear market" (falling in price); "a bear for punishment" (rugged, tough).

BUFFALO · to fool one's self or others.

BULL · (See Archetypes chapter)

CAMEL · emotions or desires in a barren, non-productive (desert) state; stubbornness; beast of burden. "Ships of the desert."

CAT · independence (but if carried to extremes may turn into uncooperativeness or isolation); someone who is a gossip ("cattiness"); often associated with feminine characteristics. *Petting a cat*—pleasure in the negative emotion of "pettiness"; concern over the *health of a cat*—spiritual progress, because of effort to raise the emotions from a lower to a higher force; *black cat*—superstitious emblem of bad luck. "Cool cat"; "nine lives"; "purr like a kitten"; to "let the cat out of the bag." (See *lion;* also see Lion in Archetypes chapter)

COW · indolence; physical indulgence; principle of natural nutrients, because of her milk. "To cow" (intimidate); "contented as a cow"; "till the cows come home."

DEER · the soul, the gentle, harmless self that is often hurt or wounded by our aggressiveness or cynicism or by other people's criticism; aesthetic abandon, because of their speed and grace. To "fawn" over.

DINOSAUR · primitive state; extinction.

DOG · domesticated instincts; obedience; can represent both friendliness ("man's best friend") and unfriendliness (they can be ferocious) in man—the positive and negative, the faithful and the unfaithful; *negative qualities*—growling, snarling, snapping; *positive* *qualities*—faithfulness, loyalty, fun loving. *Dalmatian*—black and white, accentuates right and wrong; firehouse mascot; *St. Bernard*—the rescuer; *German Shepherd*—the protector, guide for the sightless. "The dog returns to his own vomit" (see *vomit* in Common Symbols chapter); "bird dog" (to follow something); "can't teach an old dog new tricks"; "let sleeping dogs lie"; "every dog has his day"; "putting on the dog"; "going to the dogs"; a "dog" (unattractive person); "dogs" (feet).

DRAGON · the great dictator; old serpent (Satan); a strict person, evil forces; adversary; opposition to the Truth; powers of darkness. The famous painting of St. George with his foot on the dragon and the cliché "slay the dragon" both mean to get in control of all the animal forces within. *Red dragon*—the rebellious spirit; the blood stream.

ELEPHANT · power and might (God-almighty power); wisdom, sagacity, a sex symbol, because of the characteristics of the trunk; hard-worker; entertainer; insensitive (thick-skinned); traditional symbol for a long memory, but in a negative context may show an unforgiving, vengeful nature.

FOX · shrewd, subtle and cunning. *Vixen*—ill-tempered, shrewish woman. "Sly as a fox"; "foxy" (knowing what is going on).

GIRAFFE · a distortion in self, too much emotion and not enough reason (head and heart widely separated).

GOAT · tenth sign of the Zodiac (Capricorn); aspiration, because of its sure-footedness and ability to scale the loftiest peaks; aspirations carried to extremes may show material, selfish ambitions; "bad guys" as opposed to sheep, the "good guys." To "get someone's goat" (to anger, frustrate or annoy); "old goat" (lecherous man).

GORILLA · low mental state, possibly dangerous, though some types are shy and docile. (See *ape, monkey*)

HOG · selfishness, gluttonous or filthy person; overindulgence; greed. "Hoggish"; "hog-wild"; "hogging the show"; "making a hog of yourself"; "living high on the hog" (time of prosperity).

HORSE · tempestuous emotions; sexual energy; the intellect or intelligence; hard-worker. Ancient Germans and Scandinavians believed that horses were able to speak and to predict the future; therefore, horses were sometimes used as oracles. *Horse and rider*—a message from the higher realms of consciousness; *horse without a saddle*—not in control, may be suggesting to "put on the saddle, get in control"; in a *funeral procession*—symbolizes that the person will never ride again; *riding a horse well*—in control; *falling off a horse*—rejection of message. Prince Charming on a white horse symbolizes raising the spiritual energies within to the highest level (See "Snow White and the Seven Dwarfs"). "You can lead a horse to water, but you can't make him drink"; "horsing around"; to "eat like a horse"; "don't look a gift horse in the mouth"; to "back the wrong horse"; to "ride, or beat, a dead horse"; "from the horse's mouth"; "hold your horses"; "horse of a different color"; "on your high horse."

LAMB · purity, innocence, guilelessness; world-symbol of sacrifice. In the Old Testament, the lamb is commonly used at the Passover Feast as a sacrificial victim. In the New Testament, the lamb is a symbol of Christ (Lamb of God), sometimes called the Paschal Lamb. If a dream presents a lamb, it may be saying "feed my sheep"—in other words, encourage others to grow spiritually. "Lead the lamb to slaughter"; a "lamb" (term of affection).

LION · fifth sign of the Zodiac (Leo); archetypal symbol for the third spiritual center (adrenals). Although any of the great cats (cougar, panther, leopard, tiger, etc.) can represent the adrenals, the lion is especially suitable. The supreme predator; courageous; bad-tempered, or boastful, because of his roar. In ancient Christian symbolism the lion represented Jesus. It is sometimes used as an emblem of the devil, or the danger of being "swallowed" by the unconscious. "Lion of Judah" (Christ); to "roar like a lion"; "fight like a tiger"; "lion-hearted"; "lion's share." (See Lion in Archetypes chapter)

MONKEY · the irrational, undeveloped nature; frivolous or mischievous. "Monkeying around"; "making a monkey of yourself"; "monkey see, monkey do"; "monkey business"; "a monkey on your back."

MOUSE · irritations; timidity ("mousey"). "Quiet as a mouse"; "mouse-colored hair"; "build a better mouse trap."

PORCUPINE · the sharp quills could represent the dreamer's defensive state.

RABBIT · fertility; sexual desire; Easter, or an awakening. *White rabbit*—may show the dreamer the gateway to an inner world, as in *Alice in Wonderland*. "Breeding like a rabbit"; "rabbit food"; "quick as a bunny."

RAM · first sign of the Zodiac (Aries); battering, crushing, forcing something. "Ramming around" (no direction).

RAT · carrier of dis-ease; something repulsive or obscene; disloyalty ("rat fink"); the first to leave a sinking ship. "Dirty rat."

SHEEP · spiritual virtues; the followers of Jesus; conformity; easily led. To "make sheep's eyes at"; "sheepish" (foolishly bashful). (See *goat, lamb*.)

SERPENT/SNAKE · (See Archetypes chapter)

SQUIRREL · the word *squirrel* derives from the Greek word meaning shadow (low self). "Squirrely" (an odd, peculiar, or senseless person); "squirrel away" (to hide or store something).

TORTOISE · the instinctual side of the unconscious, because it lives within its shell; strength and longevity, because of its long life span and resistance to disease; introverted; a suggestion to slow down. (See *turtle* under "Aquatic Life")

UNICORN · a fabulous creature of mythology, mentioned in the Bible, Deut. 33:17, a pure white animal with the face and feet of a goat, the body of a horse, and the tail of a lion; symbolic of good will, gentleness, benevolence; singleness of purpose, because of the horn protruding from the "third eye" area; chastity, purity (it was believed that only those who were pure of spirit could see them).

WEASEL · sly, cunning, misleading. To "weasel out of" (evade commitment or responsibility).

WOLF · fierce, cruel, greedy; a "wolf" (sexually aggressive man); "the wolf's at the door" (could be spiritual as well as physical starvation). "Cry wolf"; "a wolf in sheep's clothing."

ZEBRA · a modern cliché for integrated marriages.

7

Color

The subconscious will draw on many different associations to give us direction and guidance in our dreams. One way the subconscious highlights or intensifies a situation or object is by the use of color associations. Color can also be used to express emotions, moods, and perceptions. Bright and cheerful colors may designate a person who has a bright and cheerful outlook on life, while one who consistently dreams in drab, cheerless colors may tend to be depressed and to view the world as a drab place. Black in a dream may pinpoint a "black" outlook on life. Generally, dreams with clear and beautiful colors will have positive, or spiritual, overtones. Muddy, unclear colors will probably have negative associations. It should be noted, too, that lack of color where color is called for (a flower garden, for instance) should be of interest to us. Maybe we need to put more "color" in our lives, or try to be a more "colorful" person.

The following list may be used as a guide in color interpretations. Remember, your own personal likes and dislikes may "color" their meaning. Sometimes color in dreams is used to signify personality traits, some of which are listed under the specific color. Also included with the possible color meanings are clichés which the subconscious often incorporates in dreams to make a point. If dreams persist in presenting a certain color that seems to defy interpretation, it may be helpful to consider the possibility that they are alerting the dreamer to a physical problem. The dream may also suggest a color that can assist in healing a particular disorder. In other words, the dream may be saying, "Use more of this color." If this seems to ring true with the dreamer, then more of that color vibration may be taken in through the clothing, the diet, and the surroundings, as far as possible. The disorders and color associations listed under each color are suggested only as a starting point for using dreams to enhance the body's natural healing processes.

BLACK · evil; ignorance; deception; mystery; negative; secrecy; un-enlightenment of self (absence of light); a warning; death; renunciation. "Black mood"; to see something as "black or white"; "black magic"; "into the black" (profit); "black-out"; "black market."

BLACK AND WHITE · right and wrong; good and evil.

BLUE · spiritual; contemplative; stable; calm; moody; dejected; impatient. The darker the shades, the deeper the meaning of blue. Blue is associated with the fifth spiritual center, the thyroid. This gland, and therefore the color blue, has long been associated with the human will. *Psychological need:* contentment and affection. *Personality traits: azure blue*—religious devotion; *lavender blue*—devotion to high ideals; *blue-gray*—a religious feeling motivated by fear; *Madonna blue*—obedience to Divine Will; *deep royal*—honest, loyal, and, if it contains a little purple, good judgment in handling material affairs; *dark blue*—unselfish; spiritually inclined. *Possible physical disorders:* liver; arterial circulatory system; fever; fast pulse; pain; insomnia; high blood pressure. "The blues"; "blue ribbon"; to vanish "into the blue"; "blue-nose"; "blue-blood"; "out of the blue"; "true-blue"; "once in a blue moon."

BROWN · earthy; practical; depression; negative; relates to a race (brown people). If rich in color, it is symbolic of growth, effort, a wish to accomplish.

GOLD · a Higher Self symbol; something that is valuable; spiritual graces (life, patience, forgiveness, generosity); the color of the New Man or the Father. "Golden years"; "good as gold"; "all that glitters is not gold"; "fool's gold"; "the Golden Fleece" (the quest for attunement with God); "gold brick"; "gold-digger"; "gold dust"; "golden age"; "golden rule."

GREEN · regeneration; growth; constructive; perseverance; resists change; not fully developed or perfected in growth. Pure *emerald green*, especially with blue in it, is the color of healing. The more blue, the more trustworthy. As it tends toward *yellow-green*, it can indicate deceit. Green is associated with the fourth spiritual center, the thymus, which is referred to as the "love" center; therefore, the color green can bring harmony and can act as a peacemaker. *Psychological need:* to assert oneself. *Personality traits: emerald green*—serene; balanced; determined; *pale olive green*—compassionate; sympathetic; *greenish-gray*—pessimistic; *pale yellow green*—deceitful; envious. *Possible physical disorders:* blood clots; generally run-down; ulcers; infections. Green stimulates the pituitary gland and is restful to the nervous system.

INDIGO · complete calm; fulfillment; contentment. This is the color of the sixth spiritual center, the pineal, or the Christ center, and therefore has a strong influence on soul development. *Personality traits:* good intellect; logical; enthusiastic; cheerful; humble. With a lot of purple, can indicate an overbearing nature. *Possible physical disorders:* intense pain; eye inflammations; ear problems; acute bronchitis; convulsions; tonsillitis; hemorrhages.

MAROON · poor health; negative; stale blood.

ORANGE · health and energy. Orange is associated with the cells of Leydig which constitute the second spiritual center. This center, and therefore the color orange, is the "balancing" center in the body, especially in reference to the secondary sexual characteristics. Since the cells of Leydig are contained in the gonads, orange (the combination of red and yellow) is associated with two of the four lower centers (earth centers), and is therefore expressive of earthiness and nature. It is also indicative of creative expression. *Personality traits: reddish-orange*—things of the personality control the mind; *bright orange*—mind over matter; "live-wire" type but well-balanced; *clear, golden orange*—wisdom; self-control; thoughtful of others; *brownish-orange*—unambitious; lazy. *Possible physical disorders:* respiratory problems; sluggish color; sluggish thyroid; gallstones; gout; depression; kidney.

PINK · joy; human and universal love; happiness. *Personality traits:* warm and generous; quiet; modest; refined. *Pale pink*—immaturity; weakness. *Possible physical disorders:* affects the mind more than the body; if a poor sleeper, don't use pink sheets or blankets; not advised for highly excitable people; use for general revitalizing. "In the pink"; "pink" (half-way belief in communism); "tickled pink."

PURPLE · royalty; spirituality; associated with the law. *Personality traits:* ability to deal with practical matters; spiritual power; overbearing. *Possible physical disorders:* sluggish veins; fever; heart palpitations; indigestion. "Born to the purple" (royalty); "purple with rage"; "purple language"; "purple rank."

RED · life force, new life; anger; sex; violent emotions; danger, or stop. Red is associated with the first spiritual center (gonads) and is the starting place of the creative energies during meditation; hence, red may be considered "the starter" or "the starting place." It is often the preferred color of extroverts. Red indicates a psychological need to act and succeed. *Personality traits: reddish-brown*—greed; avarice; *bright brick-red*—anger; *deep dark red*—sensual; domineering; *light red*—impulsive; self-centered; *scarlet*—too much ego; *carmine* (clear, pure red)—strong; enduring; physically fit. "Paint the town red"; "red cent"; "red tape"; "red-hot news"; "red-light district"; "red blanket" (emergency, critical). *Possible physical disorders:* anemia, lack of vitality.

RED, WHITE AND BLUE · For an American, loyalty and patriotic zeal.

SILVER · secondary to gold in meaning because it has to be polished. "Silver age"; "silver cord."

VIOLET · the color of the seventh spiritual center, the pituitary, which is the master gland and therefore is beneficial to the whole system. *Personality traits:* sensitive; appreciative; well-rounded personality; good mental abilities and judgment; high sense of integrity; aloof; self-centered; overbearing. *Possible physical disorders:* high blood pressure; bladder infections; concussion; cramps; epilepsy; scalp and skin disorders; pain. "Shrinking violet."

WHITE · purity; enlightenment; innocence; the ideal of spirit. The combination of all colors. One sees things as "black or white"; "little white lies"; "white as the driven snow."

YELLOW · bright, cheerful, full of sunshine and happiness; intuition; illumination; caution or quarantine; cowardice. Yellow is a color directed towards the future and its designation is change. It is associated with the third spiritual center, the adrenals, the "emotional" center. Mental activities are thought by some to be simulated by yellow. *Psychological need:* to look forward and aspire. *Personality traits: pure yellow*—intelligent, cheerful, self-confident, optimistic; *golden yellow*—wisdom, energetic; *lemon yellow*—spiritualized mind; creative. *Possible physical disorders:* indigestion; insomnia; nervous tension; constipation. "Yellow streak"; "yellow-belly."

8

Numbers

Numbers often have a symbolic meaning. If a dreamer is presented with a number, alone or in series, and cannot extract any meaning from it, then he or she may want to consider other possibilities: as in biblical dreams, numbers may represent time. Remember Joseph's dream of seven fat cows and seven slim cows, representing seven years of prosperity and seven of famine.

In numerology, numbers have symbolic representation. Numbers of two digits or more are reduced to one; for example, if the number thirty-four appears, the three and the four are added together, so the number to work with is seven. If there is a series of numbers such as 1893, all the digits are added together: $1 + 8 + 9 + 3 = 21$; then two and one are added together, and the number to work with becomes three. Following is the standard numerology chart for the purpose of determining the numerical value of letters.

1	2	3	4	5	6	7	8	9
a	b	c	d	e	f	g	h	i
j	k	l	m	n	o	p	q	r
s	t	u	v	w	x	y	z	

In numbers ending with zero, the zero is dropped, leaving a single digit. On the other hand, zeros added to a number give it strength or intensity (see *zero*). If numbers come up as money, symbolically it may indicate what something is costing you or the price you will pay for something. It can also be prophetic, if so determined by other symbols associated with the dream.

In numerology, the numbers eleven, twenty-two, and thirty-three are considered master numbers and are never reduced. In a dream containing a master number, it is suggested that the dreamer refer to the meaning of both the master number and the reduced number to determine which interpretation is applicable to the present situation. For additional meanings to the numbers one through seven, see "Spiritual Centers" in Archetypes chapter.

ZERO · everything evolves from zero; eternity, no beginning no ending; deity, God. When zero is straightened out it becomes an upright human, and *one* is then the beginning. When numbers are followed by zeros it adds strength or elevation to their meaning; for example, 100 presented in a dream will have the meaning of number one but intensified because of the zeros (100, 1000, etc.). In mathematics, zero is symbolic of the absence of all magnitude or quantity—the symbol for the number at the center of all negative and positive numbers.

ONE · the beginning; the one force, one power, one energy known as Universal Force; creative energy; God, unity, indivisibility, and individuality. The oneness of humankind, the power of mastership; ourselves in relation to the world; a person who holds power over us, such as a boss; the first person, Adam, as well as people's power to stand erect; the straight and narrow path. It is the *first spiritual center*—the gonads, the basis of creative energy, material sustenance, security. Some strengths of number one are helpfulness, being protective, a hard worker. On the weak side, one is unimaginative, materialistic, and lazy. *Personality traits:* the instigator, independent, and individual, a leader, courageous. On the negative side, stubborn, lazy, weak, egotistic. This number must guard against self-centeredness.

Aries (April, a cardinal fire sign), the first sign of the Zodiac, whose characteristic is the ambition to be first ("me first!"). Aries are mental in nature and should be leaders; should concentrate on initiating rather than on being original. Their talent is for beginning projects rather than finishing them; their originality will benefit them most if they set their egos aside.

TWO · the beginning of a division of the Whole; God and people, lower and higher nature; a couple, as in a love or marital relation. The symbol of duality; the number of polarity, good and evil, choices, life and death, spirit and matter; *two languages*—physical and metaphysical; *Adam and Eve*—Creative Force manifesting in human form. The *second spiritual center*—the cells of Leydig, balancing of masculine/feminine qualities. Some strengths of the two are courteousness, consistency, gentleness, orderliness. The weaknesses, being doubting, critical, shy, gullible. *Personality traits:* someone who desires companionship, full of love and service, charming, tactful, gentle; having a desire for balance; a dual nature that is the binding of opposites. On the negative side, careless, discontented, cowardly, tends toward a bad temper and cruelty. The two needs to learn the value of discipline.

Taurus (May, an earth sign), the second sign of the Zodiac, is concerned with making resources grow; material security; loves peace and calm. Should guard against rigidity, stubbornness and negativity, resistance to change.

THREE · a number of great strength because it represents the threefold nature of the one God. In scripture it stands for a completed period of time. Peter denied Christ three times; Christ asked Peter three times if he loved him; Jonah was in the belly of the whale three days; the third day Christ rose from the dead; the fig tree did not bear fruit for three years and was to be cut down; at the marriage in Cana, on the third day Jesus turned the water into wine, implying that a transformation took place. (There was no mention of a bride, and so one can assume it was a union of Jesus' Higher Self.) Jesus' ministry lasted three years. *Triune concepts* symbolized by the three—God, Christ, Holy Spirit; body, mind, soul; parents, child; Mary, Joseph, Jesus; conscious, subconscious, superconscious; fire, air, water. The *third spiritual center*—the adrenals, the use of power in the earth, self-preservation. Earth is a three dimensional experience. Some strengths associated with this center are that the person participates, takes responsibility, strives to improve, has patience. Weaknesses are lack of initiative, prejudice, envy. *Personality traits:* need for self-expression that often exhibits itself in art, literary endeavors, or the entertainment field; optimistic, imaginative, friendly. On the negative side, extravagant, jealous, gossipy, hypercritical. The three needs to develop self-control and patience. "Two against one" (being treated unfairly).

Gemini (June, a mutable air sign), the third sign of the Zodiac, relates to a breeze changing direction; associated with the mind (intellect); connects all breathing life on earth; intellectual security. Negatively, Gemini is fickle and superficial.

FOUR · symbolic of humans in the earth; the number of reason and regularity; balance and stability on the earth plane. Familiar quaternity concepts are the four fixed signs of the Zodiac; the four corners of the earth; the four winds; the four beasts in the Revelation; the four elements (water, air, fire, earth). The *fourth spiritual center*—the thymus, love in an earthy sense, love at an emotional and personal level. Some strengths associated with this center are being appreciative, generous, punctual, sympathetic. On the weak side are greed, self-pity, and jealousy. *Personality traits:* dependable, organized, loyal, logical, hard-worker. On the negative side are narrow-mindedness, inhuman, crude, full of hatred. The four needs to learn tolerance and open-mindness. In the Bible, the number forty (an elevated four) symbolizes a period of cleansing, or preparation; the flood of Noah's time cleansed the earth of corruption; Jesus fasted for forty days. Edgar Cayce predicted a forty year period for humankind, from 1958 to 1998, comparable to the forty years of the Israelites in the wilderness, the historical Exodus, symbolic of a cleansing period.

Cancer (July, a cardinal water sign), the fourth sign of the Zodiac, relates to intuitive feelings, emotional security, nurturing, hospitable, attentive to needs of others, loves his home. Negative qualities are being over sensitive, over materialistic.

FIVE · an immediate change in any activities with which it is associated. A symbol of reaching out to learn and experience through the five senses (sight, touch, taste, smell, hearing). Generally considered a number of imperfection or incompletion. The *fifth spiritual center*—thyroid, associated with the will, allowing "Thy will be done" instead of "my will." Strengths associated with this center are cooperativeness, peace of mind, subject to God's will. Weaknesses are inattentiveness, indecisiveness, stubbornness. *Personality traits*— versatile, adaptable, understanding, loves freedom and variety. Negatively, a five is irresponsible, thoughtless, inconsistent, has poor taste. The five needs to develop loyalty and patience and have a purpose in life.

Leo (August, a fire sign), the fifth sign of the Zodiac, is self expressive; when secure or mature, Leo is regal and its aura of authority is based on accomplishment; love of children; can be charming. When insecure, Leo is cocky or arrogant, self indulgent, overly sensitive; self-awareness and vanity become characteristics to guard against.

SIX · intuition, harmony, and beauty; balance or ambivalence, love that has gone from passionate to compassionate; accomplishment and growth; the cessation of movement, since creation took six days. Six adds the principle of soul to the human five. The *sixth spiritual center*—the pineal, higher mind, spiritual insight, intellect, the Christ center. Some strengths associated with this center are intelligence, seeking, reasonableness. The weaknesses are slow to learn, unthinking, and no conscience.

Virgo (September, a mutable earth sign), the sixth sign of the Zodiac, is in search of perfection. A secure, mature Virgo is efficient and perceptive. The insecure, immature Virgo type may be "harping" and perfection can be carried too far, for example, may be too concerned with detail.

SEVEN · is the combination of three (heaven) plus four (earth) when related to the dual nature of man. Perfect order; a complete period or cycle; a mystical relationship; a sacred number. Familiar seven concepts—basic series of musical notes; seven colors in the spectrum; from the book of Revelation, the seven stars, seven lamps, seven churches, seven seals, sounding of seven trumpets, pouring out of seven vials; seven knots on the rope Mohammed saw hanging from heaven; seven sisters of the Pleiades; seven steps of Mayan pyramids, Snow White's seven dwarfs. All are related in some way to the seven endocrine centers of the body, according to the Edgar Cayce readings. The *seventh spiritual center*—the pituitary, divine impersonal or universal love, spiritual healing. Some strengths of the seven are a sense of oneness, reverence, healing ability, inner wisdom, introspective, confident, spiritual. On the weak side, deflates others, lukewarm, self-righteous, skeptical, confused, and deceitful. The seven should guard against despondency and intolerance toward others.

Libra (October, a cardinal air sign), the seventh sign of the Zodiac, has such associations as a strong sense of good taste, elegance, and a democratic spirit. They are cooperative, hard working, make good bosses, strong in partnerships, romance, and marriage. When insecure, the Libra seeks others for influential associations but resents being taken advantage of.

EIGHT · a symbol of balance or cause and effect; evolution, the inevitable onward rush of time; honest, just, dependable, a leader, manager, likes activity; is strong, discriminating, self-reliant, progressive, magnetic. On the negative side an eight is intolerant, scheming, power-hungry. The eight must guard against becoming too materialistic, cruel, and misusing his or her energy.

Scorpio (November, a fixed water sign), the eighth sign of the Zodiac, is concerned with matters of life and death, birth and rebirth; has the duality of materialism and spiritualism; a profound nature, extravagant and luxurious in taste, deep in feelings, a sign of extremes, heights and depths, and the mystical. Negatively, a Scorpion can be ruthless, jealous and conniving.

NINE · the number of the Initiate; universal mind, that which brings things to an end and prepares for a new beginning. The number of mystery, the number of mothers because of the nine months of pregnancy. Literature, art, music, and the stage are strong attraction for a nine. The nine needs to work on balance, guard against fickleness, obscenities, and the like.

Sagittarius (December, a mutable fire sign), the ninth sign of the Zodiac, carries characteristics of great drive, leadership, new thought, vitality, keen, alert, brilliant, and eager to share knowledge. Very energetic and quick, with strong creative ability. Because of their many positive, dynamic activities, Sagittarians rarely express negative aspects. They may have to learn to compromise because of their demanding drives.

TEN · perfection through completion; the return to unity, the sacred number of the universe. In general, the ten relates to the one but it becomes intensified in meaning with the zero added to it. Tens are leaders, thinkers, pioneers, generally have the courage of their convictions. They should make every effort to overcome the lower level of this number which is eccentricity, ego.

Capricorn (January, a cardinal earth sign), the tenth sign of the Zodiac, consists of hard-working people, organizers, efficient, perfectionists; they prefer working independently of others but can be successful in joint efforts. They find fulfillment in being concerned with the whole, not self. Negatively, Capricorn people may be too concerned with criticism, are frustrated and frustrating by their own rules and regulations and by their eagerness not to be called on the carpet for anything in their area of responsibility.

ELEVEN · the vibrations of eleven, twenty-two, and thirty-three are of the master numbers. When zeros are added in a dream, the number is elevated that much more. It is the start of a new and more advanced cycle of manifestation; hence, it is sometimes called the number of reincarnation, in consciousness if not in body. In numerology it is considered the first of the three master numbers and symbolizes perfection on the physical plane. An eleven can be a saint or an anti-Christ (Adolph Hitler's number is eleven). *Personality traits:* spiritual, electrical, inventive, idealistic, leadership qualities. On the negative side, miserly, shiftless, stubborn, fanatic. The eleven should strive toward selfless service to humankind.

Aquarius (February, a fixed air sign), the eleventh sign of the Zodiac, denotes mental activity; the motivating force behind Aquarius is love for people, or the herd instinct. Aquarius is social, but in an impersonal or detached way. The higher, secure Aquarian is independent, imaginative, intelligent, knowledgeable, and functions best in a social profession such as medicine, law, politics, music, or art. Aquarius, when insecure, can be dogmatic, fanatically dedicated to non-conformity, and is worst when doing nothing.

TWELVE · the number of fruition, complete expression, spiritual fulfillment, perfection and completion; they have usually studied and applied and are now ready to reach out to others. We graduate from school in twelve years; there were twelve Disciples, twelve Apostles, twelve months of the year; twelve steps of service in Alcoholics Anonymous (the twelfth being that one is ready to reach out to help someone else); twelve days of Epiphany (December 25–January 6); twelve tribes of Israel, twelve angels in a Band of Angels, twelve signs of the Zodiac, twelve knights of King Arthur's round table. In Judiasm it takes twelve months to be Bar Mitzvahed, at which time the thirteen-year-old is ready to become an adult in the community.

Pisces (March, a mutable water sign), the twelfth sign of the Zodiac, is secure when he or she sets aside all the psychological and material concerns of the other signs and experiences an essential simplicity of being. Pisces needs to follow instincts and dictates of the heart and be less concerned with conventional ideas of what ought to be. When they are being their deepest, truest self, they are crystal clear, unselfish, sweet, lovable, demanding little and giving much. When insecure, they are demanding, jealous, unreliable, and deceptive. They are happiest when deeply committed to a spiritual path. They are fulfilled when they are caring and being helpful to all who seek their aid.

TWENTY-TWO · the second of the master numbers, symbolizes mastery on the mental plane. *Personality traits:* shows power on all planes, highly developed, intuition, understanding of human nature, and diplomacy. On the negative side, may be malicious, cruel, involved in black magic or crime. There is great power in the twenty-two, but how it is used is up to the individual. Pythagoras, who founded a whole philosophy on numbers, considered twenty-two the supreme number of humans, representing the ultimate test of division. The twenty-two must work hard to hold strongly to a high ideal.

THIRTY-THREE · the number of a master soul; this is the highest of the master numbers and symbolizes mastery on the spiritual plane. *Personality traits:* totally selfless in service to mankind; complete tolerance and patience, capable of accomplishing anything they desire; may possess great psychic powers. On the negative side, may be only six (3 + 3) greatly magnified. The thirty-three must always consider the great responsibility that goes along with the power of the number.

9

Sex

In a dream *sexual intercourse* (union of a male and female) often symbolizes an inner union of the male/female principles, intellect/intuition, wisdom/love, mind/emotion. It could also indicate the desire or need to integrate the masculine qualities (logic, aggression, assertiveness, ambition, etc.) with the female qualites (nurturing, caring, gentleness, sympathy, etc.), to achieve a balance of the male/female qualities. If the partner is known to the dreamer, it may mean to integrate the views, values, or salient characteristics of that person. The sex act in a dream may be a wish fulfillment, or a continuance of an evening's activities. To a sexually inactive person who previously has been sexually active, it may be compensatory. A dream of a promiscuous sex life may relate to a cheapening of self (as in "free love"). In another sense the dream may be saying that the dreamer is capable of greater creative achievements than he or she is displaying: she's "selling herself short."

A dream of committing *adultery* may be a symbolic comment about the dreamer's misuse of the Creative Force, of trying to unite the true with the false, or turning away from Divine law to a union with the flesh. However, just because the sex-partner is known to the dreamer as a married person, the dream does not necessarily fit the adultery dream category. An adultery dream will probably elicit feelings of guilt or uneasiness upon awakening.

A perfect manifestation of anything is brought about only by a union of opposites—positive (active, male) and negative (receptive, female). Therefore, *homosexuality* in a dream could signify a nonproductive situation or relationship. Also, a homosexual theme may be calling attention to aggressive behavior toward someone of the same sex, or suggesting that the dreamer integrate more of the malefemale attributes.

A dream of *incest* may be indicating a misuse of the Creative Force in a way so objectionable that it is prohibited by law (the Law). If the partner is a parent, the dreamer may be trying in conscious life to integrate in a totally unacceptable way the dominant, authoritative side of self. If it is a sibling, the incestuous act could represent an aspect or quality that the dreamer is strongly attached to and needs to break away from. Don't overlook the emotions involved. What feelings were experienced upon awakening? Occasionally, incestuous activities in dreams may be an aid in resolving childhood sexual feelings toward the parent of the opposite sex, which left unresolved could become a source of emotional disorder.

Some dreams may use *masturbation* to represent self-gratification of the baser instincts (not necessarily sexual), instead of adhering to the nobler aspirations. It could also be portraying an individual who is too self-centered and needs more interaction with others.

Anything involving the mouth frequently has to do with speech and self-expression. Therefore, *oral sex* depicted in a dream may represent the expression of oneself in a deceitful way (a braggart, cheat, liar, etc.); or perhaps the dreamer is using a gift of oratory in a false (unnatural) way—inciting riots, making slanderous statements, bearing false witness, etc.

Symbolically, *rape* represents the emotional, passive, receptive nature (female) being violated by uncontrolled, hostile, aggressive urges (male). It could be a warning that the dreamer is involved in something that is destructive to the more sensitive side of self. A milder form of a rape-dream may simply represent an unwanted activity being forced on the dreamer.

Just as sexual dreams frequently symbolize non-sexual activities, so, too, the sexual urge may be represented in a dream in a number of different ways apparently having nothing to do with sex: for example, a key in a lock, speeding in a long sleek automobile, a soaring eagle, enjoying a sumptuous meal, a pencil in a sharpener (or any pointed object inserted in an opening), horse and carriage, the trunk of an elephant. As in all dreams other images, surroundings, and feelings will help decipher the true meaning.

10

Gems and Stones

Each kind of gem vibrates at different rates and attracts different wave lengths which are passed on to the wearer. The ancients believed that gems which give off vibrations compatible with the wearer would transmit health and well-being; with antagonistic gems health would deteriorate. In those times opals were used to prevent blindness; emeralds to protect children against epileptic seizures; garnets prevented bad blood. Pope Clement VII in 1531 ran up a large debt by drinking powdered pearls and other precious stones. He recovered from a serious illness. The idea that pearls have medicinal qualities persists even today. Some believe in the therapeutic qualities of gems and stones for two reasons: that each stone has a color vibration, and that stones are minerals. Edgar Cayce cautions us, however, not to become a slave to *any* stone. As he reminds us, there are other forms of healing in nature, and we should take advantage of them all.

Sometimes gems may be present in a dream simply to designate something of value. If a specific gem is imaged and the dreamer cannot make any association with it or relate it to a personal experience, then the following properties of the various gems may be helpful. The same may be said of proper names that are the same as gems, for example, Beryl, Opal, Pearl, Jasper, Ruby.

AGATE · helps harden gums; believed by ancients to protect vision, banish fears.

AMBER · calms nerves; helpful for dysentery; aids any disease associated with a deficiency of vitamin C, such as liver and kidney ailments, diseases of throat, head, catarrh, goiter, asthma, hay fever. (The original source of amber is the pine tree, which is rich in vitamin C. Amber is not a mineral but a form of fossilized resin from pine trees.)

AMETHYST · a clear quartz ranging from purple to blue-violet. Warming to the body; expels poisons; antidote to drunkenness; brings peace of mind.

BERYL · usually green, but may be yellow, blue, or white. Alleviates complaints of the diaphragm and liver; cures laziness.

BLOODSTONE · massive quartz with small drops of jasper. Used for hemorrhages.

CARNELIAN · form of quartz; red. Prevents hemorrhages, nosebleed, purifies the blood.

CHRYSOLITE · usually olive green. Prevents fever and nightmares if set in gold.

CORAL · skeletons of tiny sea animals. Not a gem, but sometimes considered a semi-precious stone. Stops general bleeding, especially from wounds; helps digestive disorders and epilepsy in children. Brown, or dirty, discolored coral has a negative effect.

DIAMOND · pure carbon. Good medicine for all kinds of diseases from toothache to insomnia, either by being worn or rubbed on the troublesome area, or by means of drinking water magnetized by diamonds.

EMERALD · clear green variety of beryl. Used as an antidote for poisons. Egyptians used emeralds for treatment of eye diseases. Egyptian women were known for their superior eyesight. The Romans believed that a helpful eyewash could be made by steeping them in water. Hippocrates used the emerald in his healing work.

GARNET · deep red is the most valuable stone. Heart stimulant.

JADE · Orientals consider it sacred. Protects against many diseases, accidents and witchcraft; helps urinary problems, and promotes long life with peaceful end; improves and strengthens the eyes.

JASPER · opaque quartz, usually green. Cures queasy stomach and soothes nervousness.

LAPIS · lapis lazuli ranges in color from deep blue to azure, violet-blue, or green-blue. A mixture of minerals, considered by early alchemists a stone that helps attune one to the higher spiritual vibrations. Edgar Cayce said that lapis lazuli should be encased in plastic or crystal or layers of glass before being worn around the neck or wrist because the radiation is too great. Used to treat eye troubles.

MOONSTONE · resembles the opal. Protection against dropsy and watery disturbances as well as cancer.

OPAL · stimulates the heart; strengthens weak eyes. Some believe it brings bad luck unless it is your birthstone (Libra). Edgar Cayce in one reading said that the opal for those not born in Libra can be helpful in controlling temper. The fire opal can provide vigor and purification, but carries great intensity.

PEARL · since they are formed within the shell of a mollusk, usually an oyster, they represent perfection through irritation. The Cayce readings say that those who wear pearls, like those who wear diamonds, will be either soothed or irritated. Said to soften violence and anger. Lustreless pearls are considered unfortunate.

RUBY · Hindus consider it the most valuable of all gems, and it is supposed to be worn on the left side of the body. Aids diseases connected with cold; influences general body health. In India rubies are taped to the forehead to influence thinking, or placed under the pillow, to induce pleasant, peaceful dreams.

SAPPHIRE · violet. Good for eyes and boils; guards against evil thoughts.

SARDONYX · clear red, brownish red, black. Encourages happiness and good fortune and banishes grief.

TOPAZ · helps weakness of vision and hemorrhages and bleeding of wounds; allays fear of death.

TURQUOISE · symbol of youth; prevents a violent death.

11

Archetypes

There is a part of the unconscious that all people have access to, which Carl Jung labeled the "collective unconscious." It is a psychic storehouse for all humankind, and the contents of the collective unconscious are called archetypes: patterns that are found within the unconscious of everyone. Sigmund Freud also recognized a concept of "archaic remnants," inherited rather than learned beliefs, through which our basic emotions and principles are represented. For instance, monsters are a universal means of depicting our inner fears.

Again, we point out that the first step in analyzing an archetype, as any symbol, is through personal reference. A dream of drinking wine may indeed refer to a spiritual transformation taking place within the dreamer; but it might just be a carry-over from the previous night's entertainment. Obviously, if the dreamer is a vintner, the dream may be related to work.

ANDROGYNOUS BEING (Half man/half woman) · associated with the second spiritual center (cells of Leydig); a person with a perfect balance of male/female characteristics.

ANGEL · spiritual ideals; Higher Self image; divine messenger; spiritual being employed in the service of God; or an evil being of similar powers; possible death symbol.

BULL · second sign of the Zodiac (Taurus); archetype symbol for the first spiritual center (gonads); strength; material possessions; earthy desires. "Bull-headed"; "bull market" (rising in price); "take the bull by the horns"; "shoot the bull" (insincere, boastful, idle talk).

CAVE · Great Mother symbol; hidden aspects of self; deeper levels of the mind; exploring the depths of the unconscious; storage place, living quarters, area of protection of more primitive lives; site of mystery and healing; loneliness, desolation, secrecy; hiding place when troubled; a major experience which neither light nor sun can penetrate; a state of consciousness devoid of light and truth. *Cave-in*—body, mind and spirit being undermined; *descending into a cave*—a necessary descent from too exalted conscious position; *dread of not finding the way out again*—fear of lunacy.

CHRIST · associated with the sixth spiritual center (pineal); the embodiment of all divine ideas; the true, spiritual, Higher Self of every individual; the Supreme pattern set before us to conform to. (The word *Christ* does not apply to any one person but to everyone, everywhere, for all time. It was a Greek title, not a name.) *The birth of Christ*—bringing to consciousness the spiritual idea of man through the power of the word of Truth. Jesus became Christ.

CROSS · an archetype symbol for the way of Christ, our ultimate overcoming of materiality through an alliance with the will of God; humankind's fall from Spirit into matter and the need to crucify or control the lower animal nature; the crystallization of our two natures; the perpendicular bar symbolizing the inner divine nature, and the horizontal bar our material, earthy nature. *Cross with serpent entwined about it*—humankind's fall into matter and the necessity for carrying one's own cross in order to be resurrected (lifted up in consciousness).

DEVIL · all the inner impulses that resist being led by the Higher Self. (See Dream Characters chapter)

FATHER · another name for God, the Creator; provider; protector; disciplinarian, authority figure; *Great Father*—represents the guiding wisdom that comes from within. (See Dream Characters chapter)

FIRE · at its worst, fire symbolizes uncontrolled temper, jealousy, vengeance, hatred, unbridled sensuality. Its opposites are the fires of love, spiritual zeal, patriotic fervor, patience and enthusiasm; in the Bible fire generally symbolizes cleansing and purification. The element associated with the third spiritual center (adrenals); immortality; creativity; warning of a fever. *Smoldering fires*—resentment or anger, a need for spiritual cleansing (flame burns away human dross); *house on fire*—a trial through which all shall be made perfect; a cliché meaning to move fast; *embers*—possible death symbol; *back of house on fire*—hidden troublesome forces of resentment smoldering in the mind; *fires of hell*—cleansing and purification of the soul. "Too hot to handle"; "you burn me up"; "my old flame"; "the burning bush" (the Divine within that burns continuously, renewing and purifying, but does not consume); "the Phoenix rising from its own ashes" (reincarnation). (See *four elements*)

GOBLET/GRAIL · openmindedness, readiness, receptivity. Some religious practices use the goblet (chalice) as a symbol of communion with God. *Holy Grail*—receptacle for the Divine within; *quest for the Holy Grail*—the search by the lower self for the inner spiritual self.

LIGHT · associated with the sixth spiritual center (pineal); mental understanding; spiritual illumination; insight and help from the Divine; radiant energy; the brighter side of life. *Burned-out light bulb*—failure to keep the spiritual light burning; intellectually "burned out"; an idea needs to be "enlightened"; *obscured or extinguished heavenly light* (such as stars, sun)—some aspect of the spiritual life has been damaged or not allowed to "shine"; *to shed light on*—spiritual inspiration; knowledge or information. "Quick as light"; "see the light of day"; "light up"; "light in the head"; "make light of."

LION · fifth sign of the Zodiac (Leo); archetypal symbol for the third spiritual center (adrenals). Actually, any of the great cats (cougar, panther, leopard, tiger, etc.) can symbolize this center, but they are less frequently used. The supreme predator; strength and courage; royalty; bad-tempered; boastful; pride (a group of lions is called a pride). In ancient Christian symbolism the lion represented Jesus. It is sometimes used as a symbol of the devil. "Lion of Judah" (Christ); to "roar like a lion"; "fight like a tiger"; "lion-hearted"; "lion's share."

LOTUS · a universal symbol of perfection or the Higher Self. Because it is grown in a pool of stagnant water, it represents purity of the soul rising above the sordidness of the earth or materiality. Same as a waterlily.

MANDALA · designs, usually enclosed within a circle, which represent the Higher Self. They are basically a sign of wholeness.

(Subconsciously, even past lives can influence their design.) The process of integration can be seen in a dream as a flower growing out of a pot, a cross within a circle, the magic circle of the fairies; also sun, moon, phonograph record, bedspring, an ascending spiral—all represent degrees of harmony and wholeness. A *halo* (a prime illustration of a mandala) is associated with saintliness. The *triangle within a circle* shows wholeness of purpose and ideal: the *triangle* represents three-dimensional humankind in the earth; and the *circle* represents God (completeness; no beginning, no end). The *square* shows a balance in the material; however, because it is the graphic representation of the element earth (unredeemed people), it is in itself an imperfect symbol. A *five-pointed star*, as in Solomon's seal, symbolizes not only humankind's involution into matter, but also their evolution back to God. A *seven-pointed star* shows perfection through the seven centers in people. (See "Spiritual Centers" chart) All these mandalas show one's inner state and stimulate one to greater endeavor. A mandala resembling a maze or cobweb can indicate confusion or bewilderment, evidence that the dreamer needs to take a look at life and strive for greater stability and balance. As an exercise we suggest creating your own mandala by drawing a circle and putting into it what comes to mind. It can be one clue to where you are in consciousness.

MARRIAGE/WEDDING · a union, or balance, of the male/female qualities; on a spiritual level a transformation taking place, bringing the lower, earthy self under the guidance of the higher, spiritual self. *Wedding garment*—the outer self and the inner self ready to become one. *The marriage at Cana* (John 2:1–11)—since nothing is said in it about the bride and groom, metaphysically it is understood to mean the union of the spiritual and human in Jesus. The changing of water into wine (his first miracle or sign of this inner evolution) symbolizes the inner transformation of one level of our being. (The water was first poured into stone jars, representing the densest level of understanding—literal truth).

MONSTER · our innermost fears, or any negative attitudes, that are seen as larger than we can handle. (See Dream Characters chapter)

MOTHER · the nurturer, comforter; source of self; overprotection. Mother-love is our best example on the material plane of perfect, unconditional love. *Great Mother*—the cosmic womb from which all creation started. (See Dream Characters chapter)

MOUNTAIN · attainment of spiritual awareness after surmounting obstacles; lofty ideals; mastery over earthly things. *Climbing a* *mountain*—reaching for the peaks of your spiritual life. "To climb the highest mountain."

OLD MAN/OLD WOMAN · wisdom; senility; out-dated attitudes; Great Father or Great Mother images; the very old may symbolize new beginnings, depending on surrounding symbols, clothing, etc.—when something dies, something else is born. (See Dream Characters chapter)

RAINBOW · in the Bible the rainbow was God's promise to man that the earth would never again be destroyed by water. Symbolically, this is a promise that if we keep our endocrine system (represented in the rainbow by the seven spectral colors) properly balanced, the body (earth) will not be flooded by the emotions (water). The rainbow colors combined form white light—the Christ Consciousness, meaning wholeness.

RIVER · the course of life, the "river of life." Just as a river never stops flowing until it reaches the ocean, so evolution never stops until it reaches the ultimate—God. A large rolling river or crossing a wide river is a possible death symbol—cf. "crossing over." *Dirty river* (or any body of water)—"dirty" activities under a spiritual guise; *river of oil*—wealth and prosperity. "There is a River" (Psalm 46:4)—man's life flowing through his body. (See also *There Is a River* by Thomas Sugrue)

ROSE · love, beauty, perfection; universal symbol for Christ; *full bloom of the rose*—unfoldment.

SEA · (See *ocean* in Common Symbols chapter)

SERPENT/SNAKE · the kundalini, the creative life force that flows through the endocrine centers in figure eights, raising one to spiritual awareness. Jung says a snake is probably the most significant symbol to be found in kundalini yoga relative to renewal of personality. The serpent represents both good and evil. In its *negative aspect*—lust; in its *positive aspect*—wisdom. Generally, a coiled serpent represents our destructive, lustful tendencies (coil can also imply "tension"). Upturned, or entwined around the trunk of a tree, it can symbolize the resurrected power of wisdom. The ancient priests and god-kings of Egypt wore the sign of the serpent upon their headdress, symbolizing the raised kundalini, which brought to them the "wisdom of gods." The serpent became a symbol of the devil only during the Middle Ages. Because a snake sheds many skins, it is a common symbol of eternal life and reincarnation. It is the oldest Christ spirit symbol. The *caduceus* (a winged rod entwined with two serpents) is a symbol for healing.

The snake can represent spiritual power and wisdom, associated with clairvoyance and vision; it may reveal deception, sneakiness, and treachery, or dangerous situations and conditions in which one holds or expresses poisonous emotions or thoughts; a well-known tempter to evil, enticing Eve in the Garden of Eden; sexual temptations; silence (the hissing sound of a serpent reminds us of the "shh" sound). Seen wound about the brow, or with its head up, or biting its tail, it can represent enlightenment; hissing or striking, it is a poisonous tongue; in a school room, a temptation to cheat; as a *cobra*, it is deadly, and a symbol of the Egyptian Pharaohs. "Snake in the grass"; "dirty snake"; "snaky" (cunning, devious).

STAR · high, spiritual ideals; let your own light shine through. To be a "star" (having brilliant qualities). "It's in the stars"; "thank your lucky stars."

STONE · highest and most frequent symbol of the Self (because stones are unchanging and everlasting). In the ancient language of the Bible, stone often represented esoteric Truth on a literal, in-flexible level. (See *water;* also Gems and Stones chapter.) *Lapis* (the alchemical stone)—something that can never be lost or dissolved; *white stone*—a stage of higher consciousness; *philosopher's stone*—symbol of man's wholeness. "Etched in stone" (unchangeable).

SUN/SON · (See Common Symbols chapter)

TREE · support (trunk), strength, permanence, virility, dignity; one of the most frequent symbols indicating growth and unfold-ing. From earliest beginnings, trees have been connected with the gods and the mystical forces in nature. In Scripture and among certain people of antiquity, trees were a symbol of resurrection and rebirth, one of the symbols of reincarnation as seen in the falling leaves of autumn and the renewal in spring. According to the Cayce readings, the "Tree of Life in the midst of the garden" represents the spiritual centers of the body (the endocrine sys-tem). *Fallen, uprooted tree*—going through an uprooted period in one's life, unfertile, unfruitful, decadent; *tree trunk*—uprightness, strength, power to uphold future growth; *split trunk*—split per-sonality (schizophrenia); *jungle*—usually denotes confusion or an uncivilized state of being; *roots*—foundation well rooted; *branches*—branching out in life; *full of leaves*—a full life; *leaves in autumn colors*—a colorful life; *green leaves*—growth; *falling leaves*—going through a disappointing period; *buds*—ready to unfold; *blos-soms*—full-bloom life; *seed*—"plant the seed and let God grant the increase" (often related to teaching). "Can't see the forest for the trees"; "family tree"; to "drive one up a tree"; "sturdy as an oak"; "weeping willow"; "out on a limb." (See *forest, woods* in Common Symbols chapter)

WATER · the element associated with the second spiritual center (cells of Leydig); spirituality (because all life begins in water); rebirth or birth-of-the-spirit, as in baptism; emotions; physical cleansing may be needed. Deep, clear, still water often represents Truth, not truth concerned with external things but Truth about the inner self which leads to the development and rebirth of the individual. *Deep water*—very deep meaning, from the depth of one's mind or emotions; *murky water*—a destructive emotion lying in the depth of the subconscious; *clear, running water*—emotional fluidity; *clear, calm water*—emotional stability; *stagnant water*—negative emotions; *shallow water*—on the surface, or you may need more depth to a situation; *water from a faucet or well*—the water of life being received. "Still water runs deep"; getting into "hot water"; "you're all wet"; "water under the bridge to be in "deep water" (you're in trouble over your head); to "water down." *Waterlily* (See *lotus*).

WEDDING · (See *marriage*)

WINE · in the ancient language of the biblical parables, wine represents the highest level of understanding esoteric Truth, meaning the truth that leads to our highest spiritual evolvement. "Wino," possible drinking problem.

As you can see, there is an overlapping of the common symbols and the archetypes. To determine if archetypes are implied, you must take into consideration the other images in the dream, as well as the feelings and general atmosphere. A deeper understanding can be gained by studying myths and fairy tales, as well as many of the writings of Carl Jung. We also recommend *The Uses of Enchantment: The Meaning and Importance of Fairy Tales* by Bruno Bettelheim.

Jung added to our understanding of archetypes with constructs of his own which some people find helpful in working with dreams. You might wish to consider them, too.

ANIMA/ANIMUS · the unconscious feminine element in the male (Anima), and the unconscious masculine element in the female psyche (Animus). The function of the Anima/Animus is to assist the dreamer in establishing a good working relationship with the male/female counterpart—a necessary step in the development of the total psyche. The Anima/Animus may appear as a positive or a negative aspect: *young/old, saint/sinner, princess/witch, Prince Charming/Black Knight, priest/derelict.* Although it is usually presented as a member of the opposite sex, known or unknown, the Anima/Animus may be imaged as animals of every variety, or mythological creatures: for example, the *mermaid, satyr, dragon.* The Anima is almost always a single-figure image; the Animus may be a plurality of males, as a band of robbers or a council passing judgment.

PERSONA · the personality that is presented externally, usually represented by the state of one's clothes, or skin. The Persona is rarely personified in a dream since it is something we wear, like clothes, rather than something we are. It is usually a dream motif rather than a dream figure: a dream in which something is wrong with our clothes, or we are naked, or partly naked, or inappropriately dressed. When it is personified, the Persona is always represented as someone of the same sex.

SELF · the higher, more spiritual aspect of the dreamer; the inner core of the total psyche. To a woman, the Self may be personified as a *wise-old-woman, priestess, fairy godmother, biological mother, queen,* or *princess.* To a man, the Self may manifest as a *king, priest, wise-old-man, guru,* a *prophet, philosopher.*

SHADOW · the unacceptable, or unknown, aspects of the personality. It is imaged in dreams as a person of the same sex, similar but inferior to the dreamer. However, the Shadow is not always presented as an opponent. It usually contains values that are needed by consciousness and only becomes hostile when ignored or misunderstood. The Shadow may appear in many different disguises: a *foreigner, gypsy, tramp, prostitute, murderer, thief, unknown evil figure;* as an *alcoholic, drug-addict, rapist; crippled, deformed, blind;* as a *man's brother,* a *woman's sister;* a *servant,* or as *someone following you.*

FOUR ELEMENTS

The duality of meaning of symbols represents the two struggles in the life of man: the struggle against others and self. This may most easily be expressed through the four elements, described here in the sequence of the endocrine system—Earth (Gonads), Water (Cells of Leydig), Fire (Adrenals), and Air (Thymus).

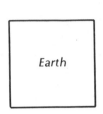

EARTH · some of the constructive symbols for earth are mountains, tunnels, ground, rich soil; if used properly they lead to higher aspirations of life, symbolized in climbing a mountain; in tunnels representing the inner self; in ground, being "down to earth"; in rich soil, which if cultivated yields a rich harvest. The Cayce readings say dreams of gorges, narrow roads, mud, large boulders, and refuse all indicate a departure or neglect of the moral way. These are often related to physical abuses of the body such as alcoholism, drugs and sensuality. Earth represents materialism, also the conscious mind. (See *gorge* in Common Symbols chapter)

WATER · in the Bible, John 7:38, there is a reference to the "water of life": "He that believeth on me out of his belly shall flow rivers of living water." The Cayce readings say this symbolizes the spiritual forces flowing through the endocrine gland system. In Rev. 21:6, we read "I am Alpha and Omega, the beginning and the end. I will give unto him that is a-thirst of the fountain of the water of life freely." Here, water clearly symbolizes spiritual ideals, which are as necessary to the purity of the soul as water is necessary to the cleanliness and survival of the body. For example, to dream of going to the bathroom is common, especially for people beginning to record their dreams with the intent of growing spiritually. The bathroom is the room of the house (your body) where you cleanse externally as well as internally. So the dream is saying in the form of symbols that you are spiritually cleansing. We use water to drink, to cook our food with, to have pleasures of all kinds—fishing, boating, swimming, etc. These are all constructive uses of water. On the destructive side, there are rivers that overflow their banks, tidal waves, typhoons that destroy whole cities. So depending on the setting of the dream, the experience and background of the individual, water may have negative connotations. For example, you could have a dream of being in a boat on turbulent water; this may imply that your vehicle (your body, represented in this case by the boat) is experiencing some turbulence in life.

FIRE · is present not only in the center of the earth and in the stars of heaven, but also in the heart of man. Fire purifies as well as destroys. God spoke to Moses from a burning bush, but the bush was unharmed. Fire and brimstone destroyed Sodom and Gomorrah and cleansed the country of corruption. Constructively, symbols of fire are the fires of love, spiritual zeal, patriotic fervor, patience, and enthusiasm. It can be soft, warm, and comforting. Destructively, fire is symbolized in uncontrolled temper, jealousy, vengeance, hatred, and unbridled sensuality. In the earth it relates to volcanoes.

AIR · we cannot live without air; it is the "breath of life," or the breath of the Holy Ghost (John 20:21–22). Air usually symbolizes mental activity. Destructively, a dream of turbulent air may indicate an overwrought or tormented mind, symbolized perhaps in a hurricane or a tornado.

SPIRITUAL CENTERS
ENDOCRINE SYSTEM / CHAKRA CHART
(Western Philosophy / Eastern Philosophy)

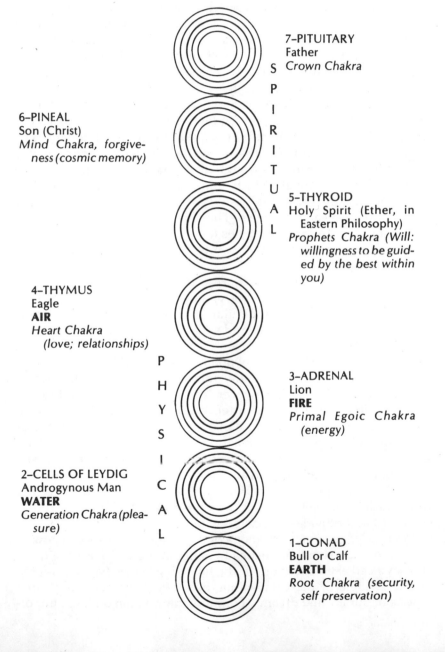

7–PITUITARY
Father
Crown Chakra

S P I R I T U A L

6–PINEAL
Son (Christ)
Mind Chakra, forgiveness (cosmic memory)

5–THYROID
Holy Spirit (Ether, in Eastern Philosophy)
Prophets Chakra (Will: willingness to be guided by the best within you)

4–THYMUS
Eagle
AIR
Heart Chakra (love; relationships)

P H Y S I C A L

3–ADRENAL
Lion
FIRE
Primal Egoic Chakra (energy)

2–CELLS OF LEYDIG
Androgynous Man
WATER
Generation Chakra (pleasure)

1–GONAD
Bull or Calf
EARTH
Root Chakra (security, self preservation)

SPIRITUAL CENTERS

In our earthly experience we function as dual beings—we have a physical body and a spiritual body. The purpose of the physical body is to provide a vehicle for the expression of the soul. The purpose of the spiritual body is to give us a sense of mastership over earthly matters and also to guard and control the perfect operation of the physical body. Clearly, then there must be some means of communication between the spiritual self and the physical self.

It has been found that the seven endocrine glands (glands that secrete hormones directly into the blood stream) are the means of communication, or points of contact, between the two bodies; they are the gonads, the cells of Leydig (endocrine cells contained within the gonads), adrenals, thymus, thyroid, pineal, and pituitary. The Edgar Cayce readings tell us that when these seven endocrine glands become properly attuned through daily meditation, they become spiritual centers through which information and energy can flow from God to humans. In the Eastern philosophies these centers are called *chakras*—meaning wheels. They are so called because that describes the way they are sometimes felt and seen; many psychics have spoken of vortices of energy at points in the body corresponding to these seven glands.

An energy, or Creative Force, rises during meditation, starting at the gonads (the motor of the body) and flowing through the whole system. The energy fills the pituitary where it spills over, cleansing and purifying the body, mind, and soul. This is the significance of the expression "My cup runneth over." This is the same energy raised during the sex act. There is only one force in the body just as there is only One Force, or God, in the universe. The use of the energy wholly on a sexual level, however, can cause sexual imbalance, as well as inhibit the creative and intellectual capabilities. The ideal condition is to have a proper balance in our activities. Dreams can give us indications of when we are imbalanced. For example, each center has its own rate of color vibration which is identical to one of the seven colors of the spectrum. If a dream, or series of dreams, emphasizes a particular color, maybe some work needs to be done on the center with which it corresponds—not the physical gland, but the attitudes, emotions, and activities associated with it.

A knowledge of the symbology of the centers can also be a powerful tool in understanding dreams by pinpointing which area of one's life may need extra attention. In the following list we have attempted to clarify some of the connections between the centers and other aspects of our life and dreams. For more information on these important glands and how they assist in our spiritual development, we refer you to *Meditation and the Mind of Man* by Herbert Bruce Puryear, PhD, and Mark Thurston, PhD.

GONADS · the first spiritual center; *color*—red; *element*—earth; *direction*—south; *obstacles*—indulgence, laziness, and desire; *opportunities*—creativity, self reliance; *level of consciousness*—security, sustenance; *dream themes*—sex, artistic pursuits. *Symbols*—the bull; sex organs; intercourse; *planet*—Saturn.

CELLS OF LEYDIG · the second spiritual center, associated with duality, balance, *color*—orange; *element*—water; *direction*—west; *obstacles*—temptaion, sexual imbalance; *opportunities*—learning balance, mystical marriage of male/female characteristics; *level of consciousness*—pleasure; *dream themes*—meeting an unknown figure of the opposite sex, sexual dreams in which typical male/female roles are altered; marriage, eclipses. *Symbols*—male/female characters, king and queen, sun and moon; *planet*—Neptune (correlation between spirit and matter, mystic).

ADRENALS · the third spiritual center, associated with the emotions, the "fight or flight" urge. The adrenals in people are larger than in any other animal, showing how much we have developed our emotions. Negative emotions (anger, resentment, hate, etc.) block the flow of healing energy. *Color*—yellow; *element*—fire; *direction*—north; *obstacles*—fear, desire for personal power, anger, aggression; *opportunities*—courage, initiative, use of energy; *level of consciousness*—energy, self-preservation; *dream themes*—war scenes, fighting, being chased, taking initiative. *Symbols*—sword, warrior, fire; *planet*—Mars (war, madness).

THYMUS · the fourth spiritual center, the heart center, completes the four earth centers; *color*—green; *element*—air (overcoming earth like birds in flight); *direction*—east; *obstacles*—jealousy, fear of loss of love, manipulation through emotions; *opportunities*—compassion, warmth, affection; *level of consciousness*—relationships, love; *dream themes*—romance, making friends, losing a loved one. *Symbols*—heart, green plants, "great mother" figure; *planet*—Venus (love).

THYROID · the fifth spiritual center, associated with the will, where you make choices, "thy will be my will"; *color*—blue; *obstacles*—selfishness, self-centered; *opportunities*—personal sacrifice to a higher calling, discernment; *level of consciousness*—

Divine Will; *dream themes*—having to choose between two things or two ways, authority versus irresponsibility. *Symbols*—the cross, mouth, or the spoken word, neck; *planet*—Uranus (creativity through destruction, extremes, psychic activity).

PINEAL · the sixth spiritual center, the Christ center—higher mind and deep memory, enlightenment; *color*—indigo; *obstacles*—other worldliness; *opportunities*—purposefulness and perspective, insight; *level of consciousness*—Christ mind; *dream themes*—transcending time and space, gaining a new vision of life and oneself, meeting the Christ. *Symbols*—single eye, third eye, light, the Son/Sun, star or heavenly body, a guru, book or library, fish, UFO; *planet*—Mercury (mind, communication, service).

PITUITARY · the seventh spiritual center, the master center, the heavenly heart; the healing center; *color*—violet, purple, or golden (silence is golden as in meditation); *obstacles*—lukewarm attitude; hesitance to serve; *opportunities*—service, wisdom, integration, mastery; *level of consciousness*—oneness of life, one God; *dream themes*—harmonious inner-working of parts as in music. *Symbols*—father, God, wise old man, mountain top, elephant (power and might, almighty power), the number seven: *seven senses*—touch, taste, smell, sight, hearing, intuition, thought trans-transference (in the state of evolvement at the present time). Each of these senses is matched with a soul sense, and can be experienced inwardly as well as outwardly. Planet—Jupiter. (See *seven* in Numbers chapter)

The *obstacles* (negative attitudes) and *opportunities* (positive attitudes) mentioned in the list are the responses or possibilities that may be aroused as the energy flows through each center. There are others as well, each linked to the level of consciousness associated with that center: for example, responses concerning sustenance (hard worker, creative, controls appetites; lazy, unimaginative, indulges appetites) are related to the first spiritual center, the gonads.

By *level of consciousness* we mean the motivations, impulses, or purpose directing our actions and attitudes at that level. For example, since sustenance is the level of consciousness associated with the gonads, our response at this level has to do with the survival instinct, the supplying of basic needs.

"SNOW WHITE AND THE SEVEN DWARFS"

We are all familiar with the story of "Snow White and The Seven Dwarfs." The king and queen of a far away land prayed for a child. Not long after, a daughter was born and they called her Snow White. Soon after the birth her mother died, and in due time her father the king looked for the most beautiful woman in his kingdom, whom he married and made his queen. The stepmother of Snow White was vain and avaricious. Periodically she would ask her mirror, "Mirror, mirror on the wall, who's the fairest of them all?" The mirror always said "Thou art, O queen" and the queen was content.

But when Snow White was fourteen years of age, the mirror told the queen that Snow White was now the fairest in the land, and the queen planned from that day on to do away with her. A huntsman was to take Snow White into the forest and kill her. Moved by pity and unable to fulfill his duty, the huntsman took the heart of a deer back to the queen as proof of Snow White's death. Meanwhile, frightened and alone in the forest, Snow White found her way to the cottage of the Seven Dwarfs, went in, saw it was in a terrible state and began to clean it up. Tired at last, she went upstairs to bed. At dusk, music could be heard in the distance, the music of the Seven Dwarfs as they came home from their job of mining. They came into the cottage and found, to their surprise, that everything was cleaned up.

When they couldn't see anyone around, they guessed that whoever had cleaned must be upstairs, so Doc lined them all up—Dopey, Bashful, Grumpy, Sneezy, Sleepy, and Happy. Doc said, "Dopey, go on up and find out who is there," and though he didn't want to go, he was obedient, and much to his surprise he found a beautiful princess. When she awakened, she made the acquaintance of the Seven Dwarfs and offered to take care of their house, to bake and cook, in return for being allowed to remain. The dwarfs were very happy with this arrangement.

When the queen questioned the mirror again and was told that "Snow White still lives in the forest with the Seven Dwarfs," she decided to take care of Snow White herself. First, she attempted to cut off Snow White's breathing with laces. Next she tried a poisoned comb, and finally, a poisoned apple which put Snow White in a deep sleep. The dwarfs, thinking her dead, placed her in a glass casket, took her to the highest hill and there kept a constant watch. One day Prince Charming came along on his white horse. He had heard about the beautiful princess in the forest. As he lifted the glass off the casket, he bent down to kiss her. At this point Snow White sneezed, got rid of the apple, and awakened. She and the prince rode off on the white horse, got married, and lived happily ever after.

Now let us look at the symbols of "Snow White and the Seven Dwarfs" in the order of their appearance in the story.

AGE 12–14 YEARS · puberty, the age of awakening to a higher part of self, the age when awareness of the creative energy is felt, makes us want to know ourselves, to be ourselves, and yet be one with God. This energy is also known as sexual energy, kundalini, spiritual energy.

STEPMOTHER · mother earth, our beautiful earthy nature when properly used; when abused it can be expressed in lust, passion, unrest, vanity, self-indulgence or many other negative traits.

THE HUNTER · habit patterns of the flesh that try to destroy the spiritual nature or our inner knowledge.

FOREST · impenetrable to the eye, the unconscious which contains the unknown, the mysterious.

COTTAGE · in the center of the forest—the temple within. When Snow White got there it was dusty and cluttered (the inner part of ourselves that needs cleansing).

SNOW WHITE · the purity within that motivates us to cleanse.

SEVEN DWARFS · the seven spiritual centers, or the endocrine system (see Spiritual Centers chart). *Mining* stands for the buried treasures that are within, contacted on a physical level through the seven endocrine centers. *Dopey*—the first spiritual center (gonads), the starter, where the energy starts to flow; *Bashful*—the second spiritual center (cells of Leydig), where the hormone testosterone is produced (male/female differentiation begins here), the area of temptation, also the area that makes people bashful of each other. At the age of fourteen boys and girls become bashful and clumsy with one another because at this point they are not truly differentiated. *Grumpy*—the third spiritual center (adrenals). The fight or flight attitude is seated here (transformed it becomes forgiveness of ourselves and others); also the Lion, king of the earth in the animal world. *Sneezy*—the fourth spiritual center (thymus), medically associated with allergies; it is also the love center. *Happy*—the fifth spiritual center (thyroid), the area of the will; in the Lord's prayer "Thy Will be Done," symbolizes the bringing together of the higher centers and the lower centers, or the awakening to "Happy is the man who does the will of God." *Sleepy*—

the sixth spiritual center (pineal), or the Christ within, the point at which light comes down from above and meets the light coming up from below, also associated with cycles, light and dark, day and night, etc. *Doc*—the seventh spiritual center (pituitary), the master gland, or the father, controls all the other glands.

WITCH · the witch, who is the stepmother, represents the use of our psychic energy to tempt the spirit. In keeping with a common mythological theme, she poses three temptations. (Jesus had three temptations—of the body, mind, and spirit.) The first temptation of Snow White is the physical one, the laces. They shut off the love center (thymus) or the breath, and without breath you cannot live. The second temptation is the mental one symbolized by the comb—it touches her mind, her thoughts. The third temptation is the spiritual one, represented by the apple, as in the Garden of Eden where it represented the fall from pure spirit. Though Snow White is sufficiently tempted to take the apple into her mouth, she really didn't accept it because she didn't "swallow it."

PRINCE CHARMING · represents the Christ Consciousness. God moves into the world to bring people out of their unnatural relationship to mother earth. It was the Christ Consciousness, acting through love, that was able to remove the apple and bring Snow White back to life.

WHITE HORSE · the King of Kings moving upon the earth. Prince Charming and Snow White symbolize the mystical marriage, that being people's love reaching up to God (eros), represented by Snow White, and God's love as it reaches down to people (agape), represented by Prince Charming. This pattern is also seen in the star of David, two triangles superimposed on each other. Another way of putting it is the unity of the Holy Spirit, or the union of heaven and earth; the unity of the Christ Consciousness and man, represented in the world as service to our fellow man. A true king and queen are servants of their people; a false king and queen want their people to serve them.

Conclusion

In our working with dream groups over the years, we have found that when people work on balance through their own dream guidance, and continue working on it, their dreams of repression disappear almost entirely. We can't always change the circumstances or the people around us, but we can change our attitudes toward them by becoming more patient and loving, trying to see the circumstances in a different way. Dreams will show us the areas in which this needs to be done.

We have both examined our dreams carefully in the years it has taken us to compile this book and have kept written records. One notation in our record mentions that on September 2, 1976, we were the only two who showed up for the study group meeting; it was then that we discussed getting together to write a dream symbol book. One of us recorded the following dream:

> *I hired a decorator to furnish a new home; every room was beautiful, colors were exquisite. The lamps at the entrance were exceptionally pretty. The dining-room table was built-in on one side, the other side had moveable chairs. The living room was just beautiful; there were seating arrangements for eight groups, done in such good taste you didn't notice that many groups; there was room for more if needed. The family room was blue with an alcove containing an organ behind a blue velvet drape; the whole room was beautiful as was the rest of the house.*

We relate this dream to the beginning of the book, and we hope we have furnished the book with the beauty described in the dream and have arrived at the balance implied by the eight groupings. The harmony was there, we just had to open the blue drapes to reveal it (the organ behind blue drapes). Once in a while we got discouraged, as anyone does when something takes as much time and work as this book did. On one such occasion, one of us had a dream in which a full-shaped tree, loaded with beautiful fruit, appeared. At no time did either of us have a dream telling us we were on the wrong track.

Dreams can tell us something about the physical body, can picture things the way they are (things about ourselves, someone else, or a situation), give a solution to a problem, provide a lesson to be learned, reflect a desire, compensate an extreme, predict the future, call attention to a fear—all this, and more. But there is an even greater value to dreams—their transformative powers. Gradually, through the months and years, as we work with our dreams, apply what we learn, and live by the high ideals emanating from the inner self, there is a metamorphosis from an earth-oriented person into a spiritual being.

For thousands of years mystical philosophy has tried to impress upon us that no person can rise higher than the level of his or her consciousness. No effort, no business, no movement, no nation can be greater than the minds and conscience of the people behind it. Prayer, meditation, self-awareness—these are tools that help develop the inner self and raise the inner consciousness. Finally, when the consciousness of enough individuals is raised to a higher degree, then the course of the community, the nation, even the world can be influenced toward noble and worthwhile goals; toward endeavors that are useful and inspiring to all of humanity; toward broader attitudes and opinions; toward viewing everything with an open mind. Current scientific research suggests that our thinking gives off particles that surround the earth. When constructive, they are picked up by others the world over. Destructive thoughts have their effect as well.

"So God created man in his own image, in the image of God he created him; male and female he created them" (Gen. 1:27). Through our dreams we know ourselves better—and through knowing ourselves better we know God better.

Glossary

Balance
> refers to physical, mental, spiritual balance (diet, exercise, work, play, religion, and study for raising the consciousness, but often refers also to the integration of the secondary sexual characteristics (*male/female* qualities) in each person. The unemotional, macho male and the hysterical, helpless female are examples of the male/female imbalance.

Clichés/Puns
> often reveal the meaning of a dream; in this book we have usually put them in quotes. Explanations for the less known ones are given. For more information on them we recommend the *Random House Dictionary of the English Language.*

Higher Self
> refers to the Divine spark within each individual, which is under the influence of the inner, spiritual nature.

Lower Self
> the earthy nature which responds to the five senses and is under the influence of the external, material world. Other terms are used to express this same dichotomy of higher self/lower self: *physical/spiritual; outer man/inner man; redeemed/unredeemed.*

123

Male/female, he, he/she
> (the secondary sexual nature) these terms are used interchangeably, referring to that part of the male containing the female qualities, as well as to the masculine qualities that are found in the female. There is no intention on the part of the authors to project sexism.

Numbers and Colors
> some qualities in numbers and colors are similar to one another. For instance, numbers ten and twelve are similar in meaning; they are both numbers of completion. *Ten* is an elevated *one, twelve* represents graduation or a completed cycle. In the case of both numbers and colors, each carries a little of the former into the next component as it advances; *one* emerges from *zero, two* from *one,* and so on. The same is true of color (consider the solar spectrum) and musical tones.

Truth
> a transcendent fundamental of a spiritual reality; an inner experience, in which you feel free; earned through applying knowledge of the Universal Law; the fountain of eternal life. "Ye shall know the truth and the truth shall make ye free" (John 8:32).

Will
> refers to self-will, the desires and appetites of the material, unredeemed side of our nature. We want to bring this lower level of will under the direction of the higher, Divine will, as in "Thy will be done."

Bibliography

American Medical Association. *The Wonderful Human Machine*. Chicago: The American Medical Association Publication, 1971.

Medical information on the skeleton, muscles, nerves, heart, lungs, skin, digestive system, and the sense organs.

Association for Research and Enlightenment. *A Search for God*, books I and II. 9th printing. Virginia Beach: A.R.E. Press, 1968.

Handbooks used in the A.R.E. study groups all over the world; psychic discourses from Edgar Cayce, to help one grow mentally, physically, and spiritually.

———. *Dreams and Dreaming*. Library Collection from the Edgar Cayce readings, vols. 4 and 5. Virginia Beach: A.R.E. Press, 1976.

Research reference books on dreams from the Edgar Cayce readings; documented case histories on dreams interpreted through the altered state of consciousness of Edgar Cayce.

———. *Gems and Stones*. Virginia Beach: A.R.E. Press, 1960.

On the meanings and influences of gems and stones from the psychic discourses of Edgar Cayce.

———. "The Meaning and Use of Dreams." *Searchlight Selections by FCG*. Virginia Beach: A.R.E. Press, 1955.

———. *Meditation*. Library Collection from the Edgar Cayce readings, vols. 2 and 3. Virginia Beach: A.R.E. Press, 1975.

————. *Psychic Development.* Library Collection from the Edgar Cayce readings. Virginia Beach: A.R.E. Press, 1978.

————. "Your Dreams." *The Searchlight,* nos. 21 and 22. Virginia Beach: A.R.E. Press, 1950.

Baylis, Janice. *Sleep On It! The Practical Side of Dreaming.* Marina del Rey: DeVorss and Co., 1977.

Bro, Harmon. *Edgar Cayce on Dreams.* New York: Warner Books, 1968.

Bettelheim, Bruno. *The Uses of Enchantment: The Meaning and Importance of Fairy Tales.* New York: Alfred A. Knopf, 1975.
A psychiatrist looks at the symbols behind fairy tales.

Cayce, Hugh Lynn; Clark, Tom; Miller, Shane; and Petersen, William. *Dreams, The Language of the Unconscious.* Virginia Beach: A.R.E. Press, 1962.

Clark, Linda. *The Ancient Art of Color Therapy.* New York: Pocket Books, 1975.

The Columbia Encyclopedia. 8th printing, 3rd ed. New York: Columbia University Press, 1967.

Delaney, Gayle. *Living Your Dreams.* San Francisco: Harper and Row, 1979.

Faraday, Ann. *The Dream Game.* New York: Harper and Row, 1975.

————. *Dream Power.* New York: Coward, McCann and Geoghegan, 1972.

Garfield, Patricia. *Creative Dreaming.* New York: Ballantine Books, 1974.

Gaskell, G.A. *Dictionary of All Scriptures and Myths.* New York: Julian Press, 1973.

Hall, Manly P. *The Secret Teachings of All Ages.* Los Angeles: Philosophical Research Society, 1977.
A collection of symbols, metaphors, and signs from all ages and cultures, including organizations such as the Masons and the Knights of Columbus.

Hartman, Ernest. *The Biology of Dreaming.* Springfield, Il.: Charles C. Thomas, 1967.
A clinical report on dream theory and therapy, with the physiological reaction during the dream state, and the importance of dreaming.

Holy Bible, The. Westminster Study Edition with Concordance. Philadelphia: The Westminster Press, 1948.

————. George Lamsa translation from ancient eastern manuscripts. Philadelphia: A.J. Holman, 1967.

————. History of All Religious Denomination. Philadelphia: A.J. Holman, 1875.

Jones, Richard M. *The New Psychology of Dreaming.* New York: Penguin Books, 1970.

Jung, Carl G. *Dreams*. Princeton: Princeton Paperback, 1974.

———. *Man and His Symbols*. Garden City: Doubleday and Co., 1964.

———. *Memories, Dreams and Reflections*. New York. Random House, 1964.

A correlation of Jung and Freud theories, experiments and cases of Jung's lifetime of practice and research on dreams.

Lewis, Grant. *Heaven Knows What*. St. Paul: Llewellyn Publications/Book Club Edition, 1969.

Lewis, Robert. *Color and the Edgar Cayce Readings*. Virginia Beach: A.R.E. Press, 1973.

Luscher, Max. *The Luscher Color Test*. New York: Random House, 1969.

Psychological personality responses to color.

Mahoney, Maria F. *The Meaning in Dreams and Dreaming*. Secaucus, N.J.: Citadel Press, 1972.

National Geographic Society. *Great Religions of the World*. 2nd printing. Washington, D.C.: National Geographic Society, 1972.

———. *Song and Garden Birds of North America*. Washington, D.C.: National Geographic Society, 1965.

Breeding, nesting, and feeding habits of birds.

Nicoll, Maurice. *The New Man*. New York: Penguin Books, 1967.

Metaphysical interpretations written by a minister on the parables and miracles of Jesus, which open up a new way of thinking.

Puryear, Herbert B. *The Edgar Cayce Primer*. New York: Bantam Books, 1982.

An excellent resource book to the Edgar Cayce readings, written in an easy-to-read style.

———. and Thurston, Mark A. *Meditation and the Mind of Man*. Virginia Beach: A.R.E. Press, 1975, 1978.

An explanation of the physiological, physical processes taking place through the practice of meditation.

Puryear, Meredith Ann. *Healing Through Meditation and Prayer*. Virginia Beach: A.R.E. Press, 1978.

Random House Dictionary. English Language unabridged edition. New York: Random House, 1967.

Riffert, George R. *The Great Pyramid*. Merrimac, Mass.: Destiny Publishers, 1932.

Historical data concerning the symbolic and literal meaning of the Great Pyramid of Giza.

Secrist, Elsie. *Dreams—Your Magic Mirror*. New York: A Cowles Book, 1968.

————. *Meditation—Gateway to Light*. rev. ed. Virginia Beach: A.R.E. Press, 1964.

Shelley, Violet. *Symbols and Self*. Virginia Beach: A.R.E. Press, 1976.

Sparrow, Gregory Scott. *Awakening the Dreamer*. Virginia Beach: A.R.E Press, 1971.
A student's manual for working with dreams.

Stern, Jess. *Yoga, Youth and Reincarnation*. New York: Bantam Books, 1968.

Sugrue, Thomas. *There Is a River*. 11th printing. New York: Henry Holt and Co., 1956.
The life story of Edgar Cayce.

Taylor, Ariel Ivon. *Numerology*. Compiled from the Edgar Cayce readings for an A.R.E. conference. Virginia Beach: A.R.E Press, 1961.

Thurston, Mark A. *How to Interpret Your Dreams*. Virginia Beach: A.R.E. Press, 1978.
Mark Thurston is an excellent teacher on any subject and he has conveyed his ability in this book.

Ullman, Montague, and Zimmerman, Nan. *Working with Dreams*. New York: Delacorte Press, 1979.
The thematic approach to dream interpretation.

Unity School of Christianity. *Metaphysical Bible Dictionary*. Unity Village, Mo.: Unity Village Press, 1931.

Wing, R.L. *The I Ching Workbook*. Garden City: Doubleday, 1979.
Symbols from the Eastern philosophies.